A Garland Series

RENAISSANCE DRAMA
A Collection of Critical Editions

edited by
STEPHEN ORGEL
The Johns Hopkins University

Nobody
and
Somebody
An Introduction and Critical Edition

DAVID L. HAY

GARLAND PUBLISHING, INC.
NEW YORK & LONDON • 1980

COPYRIGHT © 1980 BY DAVID L. HAY

ALL RIGHTS RESERVED

All volumes in this series are printed on
acid-free, 250-year-life paper.

Library of Congress Cataloging in Publication Data

Main entry under title:

Nobody and Somebody.

  (Renaissance drama)
  Includes index.
  I. Hay, David L. II. Series.
PR2411.N6 1980   822'.3   79-54342
ISBN 0-8240-4459-2

PRINTED IN THE UNITED STATES

TABLE OF CONTENTS

	Page
INTRODUCTION	1
Nobody and Somebody and the Theme of Disorder in the English History Play	1
The Text	50
The Date	63
Authorship	66
Preface	69
NOBODY AND SOMEBODY	73
APPENDIX	225

Introduction: Nobody and Somebody
and the Theme of Disorder in the English
History Play

Professor Irving Ribner, in his authoritative study of the English history play, provides what is perhaps the best working definition of the genre. Underlying his definition is his basic assumption that "the history play cannot be defined on the basis of dramatic form, for the forms in which we find it are many. Far more important than form is the dramatist's artistic intention."[1] He thus concludes that a play may be considered a history if its subject comes from the national chronicles and if its author is attempting to 1) glorify England; 2) analyse contemporary affairs "to make clear the virtues and failings of contemporary statesmen;" 3) use past events as a "guide to political behaviour in the present;" 4) use history to document political theory; 5) study past disasters as aids "to Stoical fortitude in the present;" 6) illustrate the providence of God; 7) or to explain or illustrate "a rational plan in human events which must affirm the wisdom and justice of God."[2]

---

[1] Irving Ribner, The English History Play in the Age of Shakespeare, 2nd ed. (London: Methuen, 1965), p. 7.

[2] Ibid., p. 24.

Professor Ribner of course acknowledges a great debt to his predecessors in this area of study, especially to Miss Lily Bess Campbell[3] and to E. M. W. Tillyard.[4] He agrees with Miss Campbell that the history play deals with public virtues and politics, but he also finds this view too narrow in that it ignores private and ethical virtues.[5] Similarly, he notes that the keystone of the basic Renaissance doctrine of history accepted by Shakespeare and most dramatists was that "the events of history are never arbitrary or capricious; they are always in accordance with God's beneficent and harmonious plan. Virtue is rewarded and sins are punished in accordance with a heavenly plan of justice," a view that he points out as having been fully demonstrated by the work of Tillyard.[8] But Ribner not only shifts the emphasis of the definition from these concepts to that of the dramatist's intention, but also specifically enumerates the standard purposes for which the plays were written.

In addition to isolating these orthodox purposes for turning to English history as source material,

[3]Lily Bess Campbell, Shakespeare's 'Histories': Mirrors of Elizabethan Policy (San Marino, Calif.: The Huntington Library, 1947).

[4]E. M. W. Tillyard, Shakespeare's History Plays (New York: Macmillan, 1947).

[5]Ribner, p. 9.   [6]Ibid., pp. 103-05.

Professor Ribner notes an unorthodox play in the development of the genre, specifically Marlowe's <u>Tamburlaine</u>. He claims that the providential view of history expressed by Edward Hall and taken by Tillyard as the basis of the history play "represents a tradition which, when Shakespeare was writing, was already in decline."[7] <u>Tamburlaine</u> represents one alternative to the divinely ordered universe that forms the basis for most English history plays, and Ribner notes the range of such plays "from the absolute orthodoxy of Heywood through Shakespeare's more critical, but nevertheless orthodox, acceptance of Tudor doctrine to Marlowe's open challenging of the commonplaces of his age."[8]

However, there also seems to be a further stage in this range of political doctrines or views of the universe that has not yet been noted or examined. In contrast to <u>Tamburlaine's</u> heroic or rather positive defiance of the traditional scheme of order, there are several history plays that simply seem to deny the existence of order in the world on a much more negative basis. Hiram Haydn notes that Tamburlaine is "never

[7] <u>Ibid.</u>, p. 10   [8] <u>Ibid.</u>, p. 29

really punished" for his defiance of the "concepts of limit implicit in traditional ideas of the nature of the state,"[9] and some critics have argued that he is even rewarded.[10] But this group of unorthodox plays contrasts with Tamburlaine in that they offer neither reward nor punishment, but rather seem to suggest an almost pessimistic or naturalistic statement that disorder or injustice is simply the result of worldly activity.

In some ways such a position is close to that established by the complaint tradition. John Peter notes that complaint is "concerned with man and his perennial or constant weaknesses and failings," and attacks impersonally and often allegorically.[11] In addition, two of the common themes of the complaint are the physical and moral corruption of man, and the despair and contempt caused by the condition of the world.[12]

---

[9] Hiram Haydn, The Counter-Renaissance (New York: Scribner's, 1950), p. 369.

[10] J. B. Steane, Marlowe, A Critical Study (Cambridge: Cambridge University Press, 1964), p. 63. See also Paul H. Kocher, Christopher Marlowe, A Study of His Thought, Learning, and Character (Chapel Hill: University of North Carolina Press, 1946), pp. 184-85.

[11] John Peter, Complaint and Satire in Early English Literature (Oxford: The Clarendon Press, 1956), pp. 59, 9-10.

[12] Ibid., pp. 62-68.

These themes and characteristics are present in Nobody and Somebody and do link it to the general pattern of the complaint. But the playwright goes beyond the complaint tradition by combining the complaint with the history play. The combination is a denial of the order and resolution that usually marks the history play, and an affirmation of the pessimistic or unresolved view of the world that is characterisitc of the complaint. The common pattern in the history play is for the good forces to reassert themselves at the conclusion, but in Nobody and Somebody that pattern is not followed, and such a change in the conventional form is worth noting.

Nobody and Somebody has received little attention of any sort since it was first published in 1606. Most critics have either ignored the play or have limited their remarks to passing generalizations about the play's debt to the morality tradition, its problems of authorship and date, or its lack of characterization and artistic value. Both A. W. Ward[13] and Henry W. Wells[14]

---

[13] A. W. Ward, A History of English Dramatic Literature to the Death of Queen Anne, 3 vols. (London: Macmillan, 1899).

[14] Henry W. Wells, A Chronological List of Extant Plays Produced in or About London 1581-1642 (New York: Columbia University Press, 1940).

fail to mention the play in their standard treatments of the period. Chambers notes the play's existence but assigns no particular value or importance to it.[15] Wilhelm Creizenach cites the existence of the traditional parasite figure in the play in the person of Sicophant, and the play's apparent popularity, but he has little to say about the play's artistry.[16]

Those critics who have examined the play more fully have generally emphasized similar weaknesses. Felix Schelling sees some humor in the "witticisms" of Nobody and Somebody, but finds "the main plot . . . a meagre and inartificial chronicle" that at best is described as "dull."[17] A. M. Clark criticizes "the tedious Nobody-Somebody business," "the inhuman abstractions" used as characters, and the "childish plot used of the thrice-crowned King Elidure," and concludes that "the play itself is nearly valueless."[18] Even

---

[15] Edmund K. Chambers, The Elizabethan Stage, 4 vols. (Oxford: The Clarendon Press, 1923).

[16] Wilhelm Creizenach, The English Drama in the Age of Elizabeth (Philadelphia: Lippincott, 1916).

[17] Felix E. Schelling, The English Chronicle Play (New York: Macmillan, 1902), p. 178.

[18] Arthur Melville Clark, Thomas Heywood: Playwright and Miscellanist (Oxford: Basil Blackwell, 1931), pp. 27-28, 218.

Richard Simpson, editor of the play's standard edition, has relatively little to say about its artistry, and his most enthusiastic comment is that "in construction and intention it corresponds to the better known, but not better, drama A merry knack to know a knave [sic.]."[19]

Irving Ribner, in what is the most modern and detailed reading of the play, sees the work as signficant primarily for its political statements and intentions. He calls the play "an indictment of tyranny and a warning that Kings must accept the responsibility to rule which is enjoined upon them by God," but beyond this orthodox statement of Elizabethan political theory he sees little else of value in the play. He notes the presence of "some extremely clever dialogue, but there is little else to recommend it as drama."[20]

Many of these criticisms leveled against the play are undeniably valid and the work is notably deficient in characterization and poetic development. But at the same time the play has not really received the consideration or the careful reading it deserves. Even Ribner, whose analysis at least mentions character motivation,

[19] Richard Simpson, The School of Shakespeare (London: Chatto and Windus, 1878), I, 269.

[20] Ribner, P. 246.

thematic purpose, and structure, freely admits that because of a limitation of space he has not been able to deal with the aesthetic aspects of the play: "to evaluate every play as a work of art and to discuss its particular effectiveness as drama would require a volume many times the size of this."[21] In light of Ribner's definition of the function of the history play and of the common practice of those men writing in the genre, <u>Nobody and Somebody</u> occupies a somewhat unique position in terms of structure and thematic statement that makes it worthy of reconsideration and careful analysis.

The play does deal with at least two major themes that constantly recur in the English history play, order and the nature of kingship; and it presents a rather unorthodox view of these concepts through a carefully constructed double plot that juxtaposes the history and the morality tradition while freely adapting the chornicle matter to suit the playwright's dramatic purpose. The role or responsibility of a King is central to the play and ultimately the misunderstanding of this role and the mishandling of the responsibility produce rebellion and disorder in the state. The unorthodoxy of

---

[21] <u>Ribner</u>, p. x.

<u>Nobody</u> and <u>Somebody</u> in relation to most English history plays lies in the fact that the true nature of kingship is never discovered or defined in the play, and the clear and explicit statement of order that characterizes the conclusions of most history plays is here left vague and confused. In one sense order is never clearly reestablished after the intervening period of disorder and rebellion. The playwright does present a concluding scene which superficially establishes order in the play, and there is an implied orderliness in the trial of the final scene, but he undercuts both of these positions at every possible opportunity to emphasize the continued disorder that lies just beneath the surface of the action. This artistic intention marks the play as somewhat unique in light of the received Renaissance political doctrines of order, degree, and correspondence.

The problem of disorder in the state is raised in the first exchange between Cornwell and Martianus. In a conventional Renaissance image Cornwell speaks of the sun struggling "to be delivered from the womb/Of an obscure eclipse" and the earth mourning "to behold his shine enveloped" (ll. 11-14).[22] The darkness of Archigallo's reign presents a problem that had been the

[22] All references are to this edition and will be cited in the text.

subject of numerous history plays: what is the duty of a subject to an unjust or tyrannical king? Elidure presents the standard Renaissance position by telling Cornwell to hold his tongue:

> Kings' greatest royalties
> Are that their subjects must applaud their deeds
> As well as bear them. (ll. 49-51)

This statement establishes Elidure as the spokesman for the conventional position of order in the play, and with the introduction of Archigallo and his obviously unkingly actions and of the plot to depose him, the dramatist has established a problem not unlike that of <u>Richard II</u> in its conventional structure. It is the development of this problem that produces the highly unconventional statements that mark the play as unique.

In close connection with this problem of order the dramatist introduces the theme of the nature of kingship. In the initial scenes this concept is simply mentioned and is not very carefully or systematically developed. Thus, when Cornwell, in berating Peridure and Vigenius for their conduct, says "You do not know your state" (l. 37), he implies that the actions of Archigallo put him in this same category. Such a claim is soon substantiated by Archigallo's actions in settling the land dispute between Morgan and Malgo, and the question of marriage between Rafe, the wench, and the clown. Clearly from his actions here, Archigallo does not know what it means to be King and he has no understanding of the role a king must play in maintaining order in the state. Kingship for him means "to lavish our abundant treasures/In masques, sports, revels, riots, and strange pleasures" (ll. 301-02), and when Cornwell mentions the dissension that is arising over his actions his only answer is "What's that to thee? Old doting lord, forbear" (l. 156).

Elidure, on the other hand, does give the appearance of understanding the role of the king in the state, and his statements on kingship establish him as the logical successor to Archigallo. Cornwell too affirms this estimate by contrasting Elidure's actions with those of Archigallo (ll. 37-42). But in practice appearance does not always equal reality. In filing his suit for the wench, the Clown compares himself with Rafe and claims he is the better man on the basis of his external qualities: "Though Rafe were once took for a proper man, yet when I came in place it appeared otherwise; if your highness note his leg and mine, there is odds, and for a foot I dare compare" (ll. 114-118). The King decides in his favor on the basis of these externals, but given the earlier dispute between Morgan and Malgo

and the reasons furnished by the Clown we are clearly
meant to see Rafe's claim as superior. In the same way
as Archigallo here decides the dispute solely on the
basis of externals, so Elidure is an effective King
only externally. He appears to be suited for the position, but in reality his character is not that of a good
monarch. This emphasis on external appearance as
opposed to internal value is indicative of the superficial view of existence that marks almost all of the
characters early in the play. Kings play at being
kings, queens at being queens, but there is no essence
or substance to any of the roles presented. For Peridure
and Vigenius, kingship means to

> PERIDURE. wear a crown, a crown imperial!
> VIGENIUS. And sit in state.
> PERIDURE.   Command.
> VIGENIUS.   And be obeyed.
> PERIDURE. Our nobles kneeling.
> VIGENIUS   Servants homaging
>   And crying <u>Aye</u>. (ll. 257-60)

They think in terms of pomp, ceremony, show, "drums and
trumpets," but have few thoughts for the good of the
state or the responsibilities of kingship. They do not
know the true role of a king and hence are not suited
to govern.

Similarly Elidure does not really understand the duties of being King, and rather than attempting to define the office he seeks to escape the role. Elidure has personal qualities and traits that mark him as a sensitive, generous, compassionate man, and in a private individual such qualities are admirable and even desirable. But Elidure does not remain a private individual; rather he takes on the public figure of a King, and the qualities admirable in a private man are not always desirable or possible in a good ruler. The major difference, of course, is that the king must put his personal desires and feelings second, and think primarily in terms of what is good for the state.[23] A man's personal traits may correspond well with those needed for public office, but in Elidure's case this is not so. Rather than attempting to alter his thinking or to change his priorities in an attempt to carry out his new role as King, Elidure seeks to escape the situation by denying his responsibility. Initially he rejects the office on the grounds of one's duty to one's anointed King, but when the office is finally placed on him he does not refuse it on principle or accept it as his duty. Rather

[23]Cf. Prince Hal and Falstaff, Henry IV, Parts I, II.

his actions are marked by meek wishes and a desire to return to his former position: "Never did any less desire to reign/Than I; heaven knows this greatness is my pain" (11. 650-51). Elidure is almost medieval in his desire for the life of contemplation and other-worldliness, and his position is much like that of Shakespeare's Henry VI in that he is essentially a pious, virtuous private man who is faced with the cares and responsibilities of a public office that he is not suited to handle. The problem is not that both men wish to reject this world and its activity or folly, but that both men are Kings faced with real existing problems of state who still seek to avoid the ways of this world. By accepting kingship both men give up that alternative of escape, but both fail to realize this. As Henry is primarily a King under the control of others, especially Margaret, so Elidure allows his wife to make his decisions and determine his life. His weakness is strongly emphasized by the fact that she acknowledges the acceptance of the crown and gives the orders for the disposal of Archigallo and his Queen. Archigallo, even though he did not understand the role of the King, does see Elidure's weak nature and the impropriety of Lady Elidure giving commands, and following Elidure's plaintive request "Oh sweet, spare his life!/He is my brother" (11.737-38), he comments "Crowned, and pray thy wife?" Elidure is able to summon enough fortitude to declare that his brother be banished rather than executed, but even then when told to "Dry up childish tears" (1.751), he responds "Give them my crown, oh give them all I have!/Thy throne I reckon but a glorious grave" (11. 754-55). Hence, at least at this point in the play, the role of King goes undefined. It is misunderstood and perverted by Archigallo, Peridure, and Vigenius, and sentimentally avoided by Elidure.

  The fact that the identity of the true King, that is of the king who can maintain order and rule for the good of the state, is undefined is reinforced by the actions of the two key women in the play, Archigallo's Queen and Lady Elidure. As the Kings do not understand the true nature of kingship so the women are unable to perform the role of Queen. They too concern themselves with the superficialities of the office and never rise above the petty jealousy that motivates almost all of their actions. When they first meet they engage in a game of identity that is to characterize their actions throughout the play. The Queen commands Lady Elidure to pick up her glove, and Lady Elidure answers with a question "Whom speaks this woman to?" (1. 573). Her use of the term "woman" is her refusal to recognize the sovereignty of the Queen and hence her position of authority. The Queen in turn refuses to recognize the position of Lady Elidure and her identity as sister-in-law and Lady at Court by referring to her as "subject" and "waiting maid." With a series of three questions she attempts to define the roles of all involved very carefully and precisely (ll. 575-77), but Lady Elidure refuses to accept the identities as defined and answers with a series of three irrelevant questions:

> Is my coach ready? Where are all my men
> That should attend upon our awful frown?
> What, not one near?"

Her use of the royal "our" in line 579 marks her aspiring nature and the confusion that exists here between roles or identities. The real point to be made, however, is that both women see the title of Queen in a superficial way. As the ensuing scenes point out, each sees the office only as a position of power over the other. As in this scene where the only meaning of the title resides in empty words or petty actions, so in the rest of the play the role is defined solely by whose husband is in power and not by any inner worth or nobility of character. Lady Elidure correctly calls the Queen "Painted majesty" (l. 583), but ironically she is equally as painted and overbearing once Elidure is in power. In fact she goes even further than Archigallo's Queen in attempting to establish her position by usurping the power given to her husband. She not only tries to play her own role but also that of King, and she fails to do either successfully. Her first concern as monarch is not with the state and not with Archigallo, the deposed King, but with his wife and the petty jealousy that exists between them:

>   now call in the deposed.
> Him and his proud queen bring unto our sight,
> That in her wrongs we may have our delight. (11. 697-99)

Her interview with the Queen is a close parallel of the earlier meeting of the two women, and it serves to point out the interchangability of their personalities as well as their positions. Even though Lady Elidure makes some rudimentary attempts to establish her government and to secure the state, her main concern is revenge on the Queen for her haughty insults; but in seeking that revenge she establishes herself as a double of the Queen. The point is both women fail to understand the role of Queen or the role of subject, and because of this failure they really cannot be distinguished from each other.

This theme of the confusion of identity or the misunderstanding of one's role is given sharp reinforcement by the subplot of the play. The very title of the work raises the basic problem of identity, and the playwright cleverly manipulates the two names to produce by rhetorical means a kind of confusion in his audience. On the one hand there is the obvious satirical level of this aspect of the play. If we accept Nobody simply as a figure of speech or a generalization, there is a good deal of humor in many of his statements, and quite clearly the subplot is meant to function on this level. The same holds true for Somebody, and the generalized nature of both characters allows the author to attack the common abuses of the day: "the decay of hospitality, the racking of rents, the extorsions of usurers, the offences against the protectionist code which forbad all export of raw material, wool, corn, or metal."[24] But at the same time Nobody and Somebody are more than figures of speech; they also must be physically present on stage. This confusion between the generalization and the physically present is the basis for the humor of this device, and the playwright exploits it to the full. The woodcuts accompanying the 1606 edition depict the two characters literally; Nobody has a head, legs, and arms, but no trunk; and Somebody has very short legs and an elongated trunk.[25]

[24]Simpson, p. 270.

[25]For a discussion of the visual representation of

Moreover, when Nobody is confronted by the braggart who threatens to run him through he points out that he is in little danger because "I have no body" (1. 1251).

But while this level of humor exists there are at least two other levels on which the two figures must be examined. First the playwright has raised a metaphysical question of identity. The very situation of two physically present beings playing two physically present characters who are by their natures or definitions generalized and incapable of being represented certainly raises the question of identity or reality, much as Shakespeare raises it in A Midsummer Night's Dream[26] or Pirandello in Six Characters in Search of an Author. Taken at this level the subject is one which temporarily confuses and paradoxically frustrates our minds in a pleasurable way, but there is little more it can do than make us smile at the elusive nature of reality.

But the author of Nobody and Somebody takes the question of reality one step further by tying his two vague, undefined characters to real, existing social problems and evils. This is never done in a heavy-handed

the abstract figure Nobody see Gerta Calman, "The Picture of Nobody," JWCI, 23 (1960), 60-104.

[26]Cf. particularly Act V.

or harshly moralistic way,[27] but we are never allowed to forget that one of the basic causes of the evils enumerated is that the people or the social conditions responsible for them go unpunished or uncorrected. Hence we may smile at the fact Nobody (i.e., "nobody") cares for the soldier after the war, but nobody did, and as a result many ex-soldiers were forced to become beggars or thieves to survive, causing a major social problem for Renaissance England.[28] Similarly when the issue of who is raising rents is brought up in the play, the answer given is Nobody or the equally vague Somebody. The author's point is that real social problems are made the responsibility of generalized, vague abstractions, and that no one has assigned the responsibility to real beings that have the power to correct them or who are

---

[27] Ribner maintains that the play is "a bitter attack upon common abuses of law and upon the privileges of wealth and power" (p. 246), but I do not think the general tone of the play is harsh.

[28] To be fair, many of the soldiers were thieves before going to the war; cf. Bardolph, Pistol, and Nym in Henry V. However many honest men were so maimed that they depended on the state for support, and even though Parliament tried to make special provisions for these men, the problem still existed. See A. L. Rowse, The England of Elizabeth (New York: Macmillan, 1951), pp. 196-97, 222-23, and G. B. Harrison, The Elizabethan Journals, Being a Record of Those Things Most Talked of During the Years 1591-1603 (London: Routledge & Kegan Paul, 1938).

responsible for them.

If this were all he were doing he would perhaps have made a significant social comment but little else. However, what is most significant about the structure of the play is that he goes on to unite this concept with the main plot to make a comment on the nature of kingship and order in the state. Rosalie L. Colie, in discussing the general nature of the paradox and its tradition in the Renaissance, says "the paradox is always somehow involved in dialectic: challenging some orthodoxy, the paradox is an oblique criticism of absolute judgment or absolute convention,"[29] and she adds that the surprise or delight element that is always present in the paradox is frequently based on "the incongruous mixture of paradox with a normally unparadoxical form."[30] In this instance the author has linked the form of the history play with the paradox, and the result is an oblique criticism of orthodox Renaissance doctrines of order and kingship. The paradox of Nobody and Somebody in the minor plot is paralleled by the confusion that exists in the main plot between the

[29]Rosalie L. Colie, *Paradoxia Epidemica* (Princeton: Princeton University Press, 1966), p. 10.

[30]Ibid., p. 36.

abstraction or generalization, King or kingship, and the concrete specific reality, Archigallo or Elidure. As the abstractions Nobody and Somebody are made responsible for the existing social evils, so Elidure is given the abstract appellation King and made responsible for governing the realm. But as there is a futility in making abstractions responsible for real social evils, so there is a futility in assigning the name King to a man unable to perform or comprehend the responsibilities or the true nature of the position. As Nobody and Somebody could do nothing to control the social abuses because they existed in name only, so Elidure was incapable of ruling with order and authority because he existed as King only in name.

Even though the author does not develop an exact parallel in the main plot to the Nobody/Somebody paradox, he does create a transfer of the confusion and of the implied criticism by carefully paralleling and structuring the two lines of action. The parallel subplot moves through the three realms of society, the country, the city, and the court; and in each realm Nobody finds disorder and corruption that we learn has been caused by Somebody. In Somebody's attempts to ensnare Nobody there is deception, physical attack, and the threat of murder. All of these disorders in the lower realm of the state are but echoes or corresponding signs of the greater disorders that exist in the higher realm of society and even in the heavens. The juxtaposition of the two plots emphasizes this corresponding and hence mutually reenforcing disorder. David M. Bevington, in arguing for the artistic structure of the morality play, notes that originally the double plot grew out of the psychomachia which allowed actors to double roles because of the alternating scenes of good and evil characters.[31] He goes on to point out the comedy inherent in the roles of the Vice figures and the desire of playwrights like Thomas Preston in <u>Cambises</u> to keep the comic elements in their plays even after historical personalities and political concerns had replaced the traditional psychomachia. Hence there evolved what Bevington terms the comic subplot, which acted as a commentary on the main action of the play, and still allowed the comic characters "a naturally motivated place in the chronicle play." Hence in early history plays he finds not only the structural alternation of historical and abstract characters but also the alternation of serious and

---

[31]David M. Bevington, <u>From Mankind to Marlowe: Growth of Structure in the Popular Drama in Tudor England</u> (Cambridge, Mass.: Harvard University Press, 1962), p. 17.

comic scenes, with "the comic figures, who are nominally a part of the historical setting, dwell[ing] in alternate scenes that comment satirically on the main action."[32]

The author of <u>Nobody and Somebody</u> employs this same basic structure, with the important distinction that he is no longer bound by the need to keep the two plots separate for purposes of doubling roles. The advantage he takes of this freedom will become especially evident in the final scenes of the play, but throughout the action he uses the comic subplot either to prepare for a following scene or to comment satirically on or undercut a preceding one. A comic scene occurs either before or after every major change of roles in the play. Following Archigallo's discovery of the ambitions of Peridure and Vigenius and before the Queen and Lady Elidure meet for the first time to challenge each other's role we encounter Nobody and Somebody for the first time in the country. By juxtaposing the scenes in this way the playwright transfers the questions of order and role on the comic level to the same questions on the political level. The folly and ultimate futility of trying to determine role or responsibility on the comic level of society, with the result being an almost

---

[32]<u>Ibid</u>., pp. 172-89.

bathetic deflation of the apparently serious struggle of the historical characters.

After the deposition of Archigallo and Lady Elidure's acceptance of the throne, and before Archigallo is returned to the throne there is a similar intervening Nobody and Somebody scene, emphasizing the confusion surrounding the role of King and the instability of the state. Comic scenes also occur after Elidure is recrowned and before the brothers usurp the throne, after the brothers quarrel and before their deaths, and after Elidure is crowned a third time and before the end of the play. In addition the Nobody and Somebody scenes follow a logical, artistic progression in the play from the country, through the city, into the court, and finally into the presence of the nobility of the main plot. Such movement stresses the confusion of roles and lack of order that exist not only in the court but in each level of the society, and after each comic scene we are shown a corresponding disorder or confusion in the court until the two lines of action meet in the final scene. By structuring the play in this way the playwright links the disorders in the country and the city with those in the court, implying that the nobles who cause the disorders in the court are at least partially responsible for the disorders in the other realms of society.

The final scene is well prepared for, as the problems of disorder manifest themselves throughout the play in rather traditional images according to the Renaissance concept of correspondences. The usurpation of the throne by Peridure and Vigenius is a good example. The situation of brother plotting against brother or father is one that had been used in <u>Gorboduc</u>, to cite but one example. Similarly, the failure of the brothers to rule successfully as dual monarchs is a restatement of a basic Renaissance political doctrine. The inauspicious nature of their rule is reflected in the image used by Vigenius, "Two sons at once shine in thy royal sphere" (l. 1460), a conventional image of disorder in the heavens reflecting disorder on earth. The scene of their usurpation is carefully structured to emphasize this same confusion. The playwright creates a tableau to stress the disparity between the action on stage and the purpose of that same action. The purpose is disorder, the usurpation of the throne, but the playwright ironically presents the scene in an unusually orderly and almost stylized manner. Thus at the height of disorder we find the very orderly entrance of Cornwell to Peridure, Martianus to Vigenius, and Lady Elidure to the Queen (ll. 1370-85). Equals confront equals, each entrance occurs in the same fashion, the general statements of parallel sets of characters are similar, and each grouping on stage must almost freeze in an image of confrontation and expectation, since each group clearly anticipates the entrance of the next, and the audience's attention would be fixed on the next door. The discrepancy between the purpose and the action is too great to be missed on the stage.

In the same way, as Cornwell secretly plots the overthrow of the usurpers there is the careful ordering of the nobles on each brother's side (ll. 1539-41), and the brothers are even given some political insight which allows them to recognize their need for wise advisors (ll. 1488-90), even though they fail to see the treachery and disorder within their seizing of the state. Their petty and childish concepts of what kingship means are emphasized by their initial argument over the crown and by their wrestling on the throne before the entire court. Such signs of disorder would have been obvious to any Elizabethan and are hardly less obvious today. On the whole then this aspect of the plot is rather standard and conventional.

Similarly, Archigallo's tyrannical rule is presented conventionally. We are told he is a tyrant, he shows us he is a tyrant, and he is punished as a tyrant. But with his restoration we are given a new problem and one that is somewhat unique in the Elizabethan history play. A basic nature of kingship is under investigation here. We not only have usurpation but also the usurper willfully pleading to give the throne back to the original King. It must be granted that Elidure and the nobles all seem to sense a new worthiness in Archigallo's character,[33] but even then the situation as it is presented raises some basic questions about order in the state.

For one thing the nature of kingship or the identity of the King is marked as being unstable and subject almost to whimsical change. Elidure became King because his wife consented and proclaimed "In his despite let him be straightways crowned,/That I may triumph whilst the trumpets sound" (ll. 685-86). Elidure never does wholeheartedly accept the role of King, but rather he is King by circumstance and negative acceptance, that is he does not refuse it. Similarly

---

[33]The question of Archigallo's reform remains moot as the playwright presents it. The sources clearly indicate a reform, but because of his immediate death in the play we never see evidence of his good rule. We do have his word that he has changed (ll. 1018-21), but such a testimony is hardly conclusive in the light of his earlier actions and statements (l. 750). Ribner concludes that Archigallo's "further tyranny is cut off by death" (p. 245), but I feel the question is purposefully left open-ended to emphasize the changing, confused nature of the throne.

Archigallo became King again simply because he happened to be found in the woods by his brother. The transient nature of kingship is emphasized throughout this encounter. Archigallo sets this tone with his initial statement "I was a king, but now I am a slave" (l. 903). That a similar switch might occur again is stressed by the echoing statements

> ARCHIGALLO. I was a King.
>
> ELIDURE. And I may be a wretch. (ll. 922-23)

Indeed, Cornwell does not even recognize Archigallo when he meets him, but because Elidure does and because Archigallo has evidently undergone a change of character, he is quickly made King again. However, his triumph is shortlived, for within a hundred lines of Malgo's announcement that Archigallo is King, Martianus announces his death and Elidure's return to the throne.

The changes that the playwright has made in his sources on this point are significant. Both Geoffrey of Monmouth and Holinshed are possible sources for the play, and critics are divided on which is primary. If we accept Monmouth as the basic source, as do Simpson[34] and Ribner,[35] the playwright has made some striking alterations in the details of the legend. For example Monmouth

---

[34] Simpson, p. 269   [35] Ribner, p. 244.

notes a reign of five years for Elidure before Archigallo is found and made King.[36] Also Archigallo had been trying to raise help to take his throne back by force. Perhaps the most interesting difference between the source and the play is that in Monmouth's account the nobles accept Archigallo as King only under force. Elidure hides Archigallo, feigns sickness to attract the nobles to his palace, and then one by one forces each noble to accept Archigallo under penalty of death. In addition Archigallo then rules well for ten years before he dies, punishing evil and rewarding those who were virtuous.

If we accept Holinshed as the source, as does Schelling,[37] the differences are not as dramatic, but they are significant. Holinshed emphasizes Elidure's good and just rule, noting that he constantly worked to get his brother back on the throne, as he felt it was the just thing to do.[38] He wins the noble's consent to

[36] "Geoffrey on Monmouth's British History," Old English Chronicles, ed. J. A. Giles (London: G. Bell and Sons, 1912), pp. 134-35.

[37] Schelling, p. 187

[38] Holinshed's Chronicles of England, Scotland and Ireland, 3 vols. (London: printed for J. Johnson, 1807-08), I, 459-61.

restore Archigallo not by force, but "with wise and discreet words," after having governed well for three years, and Archigallo then proves a worthy and just King loved by all his subjects.

Even though the playwright seems to have been following Monmouth as his primary source, either historical account shows that he consciously omitted the intervening good rule of Elidure and the subsequent rule of Archigallo. Had he included the details of Elidure's successful rule our opinion of Elidure would have been heightened and strengthened; however, by omitting such details the playwright leaves our attitude toward Elidure vague at best. He does have virtues, but without these details there is little evidence that the virtues are kingly or produce a stable reign. The omission of Archigallo's successful reign emphasizes the instability of the throne and the indeterminate nature of the kingship. As outlined in the play the restoration is not the result of wise, rational counsel or discussion, or even of a careful plan of force and intimidation, but rather of an accidental meeting. By choosing to omit the details of the restoration and of the two reigns the playwright emphasizes the whimsical or almost chance nature of the change in power, and thus undermines the stability of or respect for the throne. The identity of the King may change from moment to moment and hence cannot be very clearly defined.

The confused state of the throne and of the kingdom, and the impropriety of the relationship existing between subject and sovereign are underscored by the conduct of the two Queens in this scene. Their actions could almost be comical if the matters at hand were not the most serious subjects and values dealt with in the English history play. Instead of being comic they deflate the return to power of Archigallo and belittle his death and the rise of Elidure by their actions and comments. Prior to Cornwell's entrance Archigallo's Queen has been revelling in her restored position of power over Lady Elidure. The confused nature of the throne is emphasized by Cornwell's opening question, "Where's the queen?" (l. 1119), which also might be taken as asking who is the Queen.[39] The disorder that exists in the state is also sharply pointed out by Lady Elidure's reaction to the news that Archigallo is ill: "Now if it be thy will, sweet blessed heaven,/Take him to mercy" (ll. 1123-24). We might say this is simply Lady Elidure expressing her great desire to be in a position of power, but Archigallo is her King, and she is openly calling on

[39] Cf. Richard II, "God save the King! Will no man say amen?" (IV.i.172).

heaven to take his life. She continues her disdainful attitude when called upon to help the Queen who has fainted: "I'll see her burst first" (l. 1132). The Queen's reactions are equally shameful and disorderly. She does swoon and is greatly affected by the news, but her reactions are not for her husband and not even for her King, but for herself: "I had rather die/Than lose the title of my sovereignty" (ll. 1134-35). Her mind is fixed on her petty quarrel with Lady Elidure and she never does express any sorrow at the fact that she is now a widow and her sovereign is dead. The only hint at sorrow is delivered by Lady Elidure in a statement filled with irony and the shallowness of the scene:

> Yet we'll stay our rage,
> We will forbear our spleen, for charity
> And love unto the dead, till you have hearsed
> Your husband's bones. (ll. 1136-39)

Neither woman understands the role of subject, wife, or Queen, and this lack of decorum or failure to understand is indicative of the confused nature of the entire state.

Nor does the state suddenly take on a new order and stability with the lawful coronation of Elidure. When he first came to power Malgo had said he was "the very soul of lenity" and had ascribed to him the "virtue" of "moderation" (ll. 638-40). Lady Elidure, on the other hand, had called his characteristic actions "mildness" and had scorned this trait as a weakness rather than a strength. Indeed, even though she does not understand herself or the state she does see her husband accurately, at least in this trait. This same weakness of character is also mentioned by Cornwell earlier in the play (l. 239) and even Peridure and Vigenius use this point in defense of their usurpation of the throne:

> 'Twas not ambition or the love of state
> That drew us to this business, but the fear
> Of Elidurus' weakness. (ll. 1491-93)

What begins in Elidure as the desire for "the middle path, the golden mean" (l. 662) becomes instead the excess of his abdication and his desire for the quiet, contemplative life in the face of responsibility. His greatest joy at the restoration of his brother is that it "takes from me a kingdom's cares away" (l. 1017).

Similarly the statements that he makes early in the play upholding order as the most important attribute of the state pale next to his actions as King. When he chooses to give up his throne to Archigallo he says "I am loved, I know" (l. 966), and Morgan supports his statement: "happy is Britain/Under the government of Elidure" (ll. 976-77). Yet these statements too are empty in the face of evidence. Britain is not happy, as the reports of Nobody and Somebody clearly indicate. Britain is not happy when the same man who claimed she was suddenly enters without explanation, announces that he is part of the plot to overthrow Elidure, and proudly proclaims "Two thousand soldiers have I brought from Wales/To wait upon the princely Peridure" (ll. 1329-30). Given the characters of Peridure and Vigenius it is not unusual that they rebel, but what is significant is that Morgan and Malgo, trusted nobles of the court, lead the conspiracy along with Archigallo's Queen. Only Cornwell (and probably Martianus) remain unquestionably loyal to Elidure throughout the usurpation, and the state can hardly be happy and stable with intrigues of this sort at hand.

But what is even more amazing and singular about this play is that even after the rebellion defeats itself there is at best only a superficial and perfunctory return to order within the state. The normal pattern followed in the history play calls for a return to stability and hence a reaffirmation of universal order following a rebellious interlude. As Tillyard has pointed out this is perhaps the most important statement made in Shakespeare's two history cycles. But here the playwright merely creates a surface appearance of orderliness and then takes special pains to point out the disorder that remains just below that surface. Again a comparison with the sources is significant. The playwright omits the details that would in any way tend to justify the rebellion or suggest a return to order or a stable government, and emphasizes those points which stress the weaknesses of Elidure and the confusion and disorder of the realm. Monmouth almost excuses the rebellion and ignores the political implications of usurpation. In his account the brothers rule jointly for seven years until Vigenius dies of natural causes. Peridure then governs "with generosity and mildness, so that he even excelled his other brothers who had preceded him," until "Fate removed him suddenly," and the forgotten Elidure is released from prison, crowned, and finishes his life in just and virtuous actions.

Holinshed claims that the brothers revolted out of envy and malice, and goes on to note a confusion in historical accounts as to how they divided their rule. In any event, he agrees with Monmouth that Vigenius died first and that Peridure then ruled the land well, but he adds that "others write that he was a verie tyrant, and used himselfe verie cruellie towards the lords of his land, whereupon they rebelled and slue him." Holinshed does not choose between these varying accounts of

Peridure's rule, but he does note Elidure's return to the throne and his just rule.

By choosing to compress the rule of the two brothers into a few minutes and to have them slay each other in an argument about who should rule, the playwright again emphasizes the undefined and instable nature of the throne and the disorder of the realm. There are no hints that the brothers are even capable of a just rule, and their excuse for usurping the throne (ll. 1491-94) is feeble at best. Moreover the playwright chooses to take the primary responsibility for the rebellion out of the hands of the brothers and give it to Archigallo's Queen, a completely unhistorical personage. From Vigenius' comments it is evident that the plot was her idea and that she is planning the actions (ll. 1295-98). Again she clearly states "All that I crave/Is but to make the imperious queen my slave" (ll. 1311-12), but nevertheless she is at the head of the conspiracy. However, following the deaths of the brothers and hence the defeat of the rebellion, she is welcomed into the court by the new King as if all her past wrongs had simply been forgotten:

> My loved queen! Come, seat thee by my side,
> Partner in all my sorrows and my joys;
> And you, her reconciled sister, sit

By her in second place of majesty.

It joys me that you have outworn your pride.

(ll. 1793-97)

The reconciliation of the two women, however, has been as shallow and essentially meaningless as was their initial jealousy. Sicophant, the character who is used throughout the play to mark the frequent changes in fortune of the women and the folly of the change, reconciles them in a weak scene by double threats of murder, a lie of good will, and threats of imminent changes of fortune (ll. 1690-1776). In short, their basis for reconciliation is no more substantial than their basis for quarreling and hence should not deserve much credence. But Elidure accepts the reconciliation at full face value, and no mention is made of the disorder prompted by the Queen. To ignore the disorder is to deny the traditional pattern followed in history plays for crimes against the state.

In like manner Elidure's responses to the brothers' demands that he resign the throne are singularly unkingly. In an excessively rhetorical speech he bemoans the cares of the office and expresses relief that "this great charge" (l. 1435) will be lifted from him. Moreover, he praises their "able loins" (l. 1433), refers to them as "kind youths" (l. 1436), and concludes "Here, take my crown" (l. 1438). When upbraided by his wife for his weak defense of his position he responds

> Thinkst thou I praise my crown above thy life?
> No, take it lords, it hath my trouble been,
> And for this crown, oh give me back my queen.
>
> (ll. 1444-46)

Such sentiments may show his virtue and his lack of selfish ambition, but they hardly mark him as an anointed monarch whose first duty is to the order of the state; rather they serve to underline his poor conception of the role of the King.

His attitude toward the brothers following his return to power is equally unconventional. Instead of condemning their actions or pointing them out as examples of ill conceived ambition, he wishes "with all my soul" that his brothers had not died and says "But we have given them honorable graves,/And mourned their most untimely funeral" (ll. 1791-92). If anything their funeral was most timely for the good of the state, and even though they died young, to bury unrepentant and unreformed usurpers honorably is to ignore or even to deny their guilt and disorderly conduct. It is almost as if the convention is being reversed to emphasize the disorder of the realm.[40]

---

[40]The best discussion of such conventions in Elizabethan

The only explanation given for such actions is delivered by Malgo following the deaths of Peridure and Vigenius, in the presence of Morgan and Martianus, and in response to Cornwell's query

> Yet we are enemies; why fight we not
> With one another for our generals' loss?
> MARTIANUS. Too much blood already hath been spent.
> Now, therefore, since the difference in themselves
> Is reconciled in either's overthrow,
> Let us be as we were before this jar,
> And joining hands like honorable friends,
> Inter their bodies as becomes their state.
> (ll. 1677-84)

However this speech is not enough to justify Elidure's actions. For one thing, Malgo is a traitor to the state. Cornwell's question points out the shallowness of their tie to the brothers, but nevertheless both Malgo and Morgan had plotted the overthrow of the King. Hence it is certainly to their advantage to forget differences and act as if nothing had happened or "as we were before this jar."

Secondly, the crimes involved here are major, the

drama is Theodore Spencer, <u>Death and Elizabethan Tragedy</u> (Cambridge, Mass.: Harvard University Press, 1936).

most dangerous crimes that can be committed against the state: usurpation and the threat of regicide. The very enormity of the acts demands more treatment and justification than simply one speech by one of the conspirators. Moreover, even if Malgo were not involved in the crime, it is the place and duty of the King to pass judgment on those involved and to pardon or punish them as he sees fit. In this case, however, no such judgment is ever made, and instead the incident is allowed to slip into the background. Malgo and Morgan remain unpunished and resume their places at court by Elidure's consent. Cornwell and Martianus, the two who have been most faithful to the order of the state (ll. 1396-1424) are not without taint either, as they tacitly accept the arrangement and choose to overlook the wrongs that have been done. And, in addition, they were indirectly responsible for the deaths of the two brothers, as they goaded them into fighting over the treatment of the Queen; hence to voice concern for burying them with proper respect and ceremony is at least hypocritical. Thus the corruption and disorder that characterized the rebellion are never cleared from the court, and they still exist beneath the veneer of forgiveness and stability that Elidure tries to maintain.

We might argue that unfinished elements of this sort in the play are simply due to the carelessness or lack of ability of the playwright, but the overall structure, the changes in the source, and the accumulation of consistent details supporting the position of disorder seem to point to a consciously artistic work. This purposive design is dramatically brought to light by combining the two plots of the play for the first time. The dramatist has cleverly moved the Somebody-Nobody plot into the court, and the trial of Nobody reflects not only the disorder that is present but also the failure of everyone present to see themselves for what they truly are.

It is significant that the first mingling of the two plots involves a meeting between Somebody and Sicophant. Both characters are concerned with their own good, and both are willing to go to any lengths to achieve what they want. As Somebody will lie, hire, and plot to ensnare Nobody, so Sicophant will jump to whichever side is in power or favor to achieve reward. It is also interesting that they teach each other something, Somebody explaining how to use crooked dice and Sicophant demonstrating how to cheat at cards. They each represent the vice and corruption of their respective realms, but one is not necessarily any worse or better than the other.

This point is well illustrated by the trial, which is the climactic scene of the play. Here the playwright cleverly fuses the problem of the nature of kingship with the disorder of the state by accusing Nobody of the crimes, not only of the country and the city, but also of the court. In terms of the country and city crimes we have seen that they were perpetrated by Somebody and blamed on Nobody on a figurative level of the play. It is also clear that figuratively blaming the crimes on Nobody or Somebody is tantamount to ignoring the true causes or persons responsible for them, since Nobody and Somebody are noncorporeals who cannot be punished. There is some difference between charging Nobody with the guilt and charging Somebody, since Somebody does denominate some guilty party, however generally, and within the paradox that the playwright has established, Somebody may seem to have existence and to be capable of effective guilt. But in reality he is as equally elusive as Nobody in that he designates no single, specific party who can be charged with meaningful responsibility. What the trial does then is to take the blame for the real problems of disorder in the realm of the court away from the persons physically present at court and transfer it to the figurative and abstract characters of Nobody and Somebody. The trial then of Nobody becomes a sham and a mockery of the trial of the traitors that should have taken place if order were to be restored.

Following Elidure's announcement of the noble treatment of the brothers and the reconciliation of the women, any further discussion or explanation of the matter is cut off by Elidure's question "My Lord of Cornwell, who's that whispers to you?" (1. 1802). Cornwell's answer that the contention between Nobody and Somebody has come to court marks the substitution of that problem for the more important issues that had been at hand. Ironically the trial gives a superficial sense of order to the ending of the play. Elidure speaks and acts here in an orderly and efficient manner, using the royal we, making a clear decision, and issuing orders: "We'll sit in person on their controversies./Admit them Cornwell" (11. 1811-12). Such a trial to establish justice might easily occur in a standard English history play, but here all is not neatly concluded, and the playwright purposefully sets up this false position of order to contrast with the disorder that is more deeply present in the play. The irony lies in the real order of the sham trial as opposed to the sham order of the real trial that never occurs. The almost absurd answers of Nobody and Somebody to the King's questions serve to undercut and expose the folly of the pretended ceremony:

SOMEBODY. I beg against this fellow,
Justice, my liege.

ELIDURE.   Against whom?

SOMEBODY.   Against Nobody.

(ll. 1826-27)

Surely the scene is meant to be humorous, and the humor of the situation should not be missed. But behind the laughter there still hangs the seriousness of the crimes committed in the court, as well as the injustices that exist in the country and the city, and we as readers or viewers are not allowed to forget them; the indictment read against Nobody serves to call the wrongs to mind.

Nobody cleverly acquits himself of the crimes in the country with a logical twist: "If things were done, they must be done by Somebody,/Else could they have no being" (ll. 1884-85). We certainly may smile at his wit, but the crimes of the country still exist and no effectual guilt has been charged.

Nobody uses the same type of reasoning to escape from the crimes of the city, but here an interesting thing occurs. The accusations of the crimes of the country were carried on primarily by Somebody, with a single comment from Martianus, two comments from Elidure, and three from Cornwell. When Nobody appears free from guilt in the country Sicophant urges that he be tried for the city crimes (ll. 1909-10). The Queen interrupts Somebody's accusations and says "Though he hath cleared himself from country crimes./He cannot scape the city" (ll. 1925-26). Following his defense against these charges, Sicophant says "If neither city nor country will prevail, to him with the court Master Somebody, and there you will match him" (ll. 1951-53). At this point all the members of the court are quite ready to accuse Nobody and to join in the prosecution. Cornwell charges him with "libels 'gainst the state" (l. 1956), Martianus with "strange rumors and false buzzing tales/ Of mutinous leesings," Malgo with "False dice and cheating," and Morgan with "Cards of advantage." All seem quite content on prosecuting Nobody, but all ignore the real crimes against the state and their own guilt. It is almost as if a scapegoat is needed here and Nobody is convenient. When Nobody proves his innocence, Somebody and Sicophant are convicted, and they may now serve as expiatory agents for the disorder of the realm. Elidure's vengeance is swift and sure. Cornwell sets the tone for punishment:

> My liege, you cannot be too severe in punishing
> Those monstrous crimes, the only stain and blemish
> To the weal public. (ll. 2001-03)

A relatively mild punishment is given to Sicophant, and

Morgan, Malgo, and Lady Elidure all take part in sentencing him. Sicophant's role throughout the play is obvious and accepted. Several characters had commented on and condemned his changing his allegiance to fit the occasion (ll. 1041-44), but he is tolerated and allowed to maintain his position at court. Ironically only Peridure and Vigenius banish him from the field before their battle (ll. 1655-58), while more conventional characters supposedly representing order tolerate his fawning hypocrisy. Yet in this scene all suddenly condemn what they had tacitly condoned before. The venom of Lady Elidure's statement is particularly noticeable:

> Let me doom him; smooth spaniel, soothing groom,
> Slick, oily knave, egregious parasite!
> Thou turning vane and changing weathercock,
> My sentence is thou shalt be naked stripped
> And by the city beadles soundly whipped. (ll. 2021-25)

Somebody is given an even severer penalty for his crimes directly against the state, and his punishment is delivered by the King:

> All that thou hast is forfeit to the law.
> For thy extortion, I will have thee branded
> Upon the forehead with the letter F;
> For cheating, whipped; for forging, lose thine ears;

>   Last, for abasing of thy sovereign's coin
>
>   And traitrous impress of our kingly seal,
>
>   Suffer the death of traitors. (ll. 2006-12)

However, neither punishment restores order to the state. Both are symbolic punishments, and again the paradox creates the illusion that a real party (i.e. a "somebody") is being punished, rather than no one at all. But Somebody is figurative and has no individuality or effective existence. Hence to punish Somebody is to punish anybody and hence to punish nobody. In the same way Sicophant really has no major or significant identity in the court. He served whoever was at hand and in power, and hence by being any man's man he was no man's man. His punishment then is mere tokenism and serves only to remind us of the greater crimes that have gone unpunished. Elidure takes a strong stand in support of justice and order in the state for the first time since his early speeches, but his position is merely a pose, and the identity of the King here is no clearer than is the identity of those responsible for the wrongs of the country or the city or even the court, for those guilty in the court hide behind the mask of righteous indignation. The playwright has thus created a scene that might occur at the end of a conventional history play, but he has so undercut the conventions of the trial, the prosecution, and the sentencing with hypocrisy, meaningless actions, and disorder that he destroys the firm affirmation of order and control that is an essential part of the traditional form. Rather than creating a sense of finality and stability, he leaves us thinking of the wrongs that have gone unpunished and looking at the potential for the next rebellion in the hastily reconciled Queens, the questionably loyal counsellors, and the vacillating King.

In his first appearance on stage Somebody charges his servant with the goals he wants to accomplish in the land:

> Bring scandals on the rich, raise mutinous lies
> Upon the state and rumors in the court,
> Backbite and sow dissention amongst friends,
> Quarrels mongst neighbors, and debate mongst strangers,
> Set man and wife at odds, kindred at strife.
>   (11. 367-71)

Essentially all of these elements of disorder have occurred, but they have not been meaningfully obviated. Justice, "the prime virtue of the King,"[41] has been left wanting. Even though Nobody is freed and Somebody is

---

[41] Ernest W. Talbert, The Problem of Order (Chapel Hill: University of North Carolina Press, 1962), p. 12.

punished, somebody deposed the king and created disorder in the realm, and nobody is punished for that. Elidure may have been "Three sundry times crowned king of this fair land" (1. 2049), but all of the crowns are hollow.

The Text

The play <u>Nobody and Somebody</u> was entered in the Stationer's Register by John Trundle, the publisher and bookseller, on March 12, 1606, and was subsequently published that same year in a quarto edition.[42] There is no extant manuscript.

Following the English publication, the play appears in manuscript in Graz, Austria (1608),[43] "dedicated to the Grandduke Maximilian, brother of Emperor Ferdinand II, and signed by John Green, one of the wandering English Comedians who toured in Germany during the first quarter of the seventeenth century."[44] This

---

[42] On January 8, 1606, "The picture of No bodye" was entered in the Stationer's Register to John Trundell. The printer has not been identified.

[43] This manuscript is currently in the library of the Cistercian Monastery at Rein, in Steiermark, Austria.

[44] F. J. Kramer, <u>Dissertation Abstracts of the Ohio State University</u> (Columbus: Ohio State University, 1963), p. 61. For a more complete history of the English Comedians in Germany see Albert Cohn, <u>Shakespeare in Germany in the Sixteenth and Seventeenth Centuries</u> (1865; rpt. Wiesbaden, Germany, Dr. Martin Sandis oHG, 1967); see also Charles Harris, "English Actors in Germany in the

manuscript is almost certainly "a fair copy of a dictated prototype," according to F. J. Kramer, the most recent editor of the manuscript.[45] He surmises that the manuscript is a memorial reconstruction of the English play, dictated by Green and copied by a German scribe of Chancery. He cites as evidence to support such a conclusion (1) the German dialect of the manuscript which Green and his troupe could not have known, (2) errors that strongly suggest mistakes in hearing dictation, (3) corrected errors and interlineations that indicate a fair copy.[46] It is highly unlikely that the English Comedians, who probably left London and went into Germany because they could not find work on the English stage, would have brought some sort of manuscript or prompt copy with them.[47] Such materials were the property of established dramatic companies, and since the companies traveling on the continent were splinter or vagabond groups of unemployed actors, it is improbable that they would have possessed such works. Green might

---

16th and 17th Centuries," <u>Western Reserve University Bulletin</u>, 10 (1907), 136-163.

[45] F. J. Kramer, "The Origin of the Manuscript Version of Niemand und Jemand," <u>Monatshefte fur Deutschen Unterricht</u>, 37 (April-May, 1945), 85-95

[46] <u>Ibid</u>. Kramer also includes a fuller discussion of the circumstances surrounding the dictating of the manuscript.

[47] Cohn, pp. xx-xxi.

have seen a manuscript of the English play, but it is far more likely that he witnessed a production by Queen Anne's players, and that that experience became the basis for his German version.[48] The manuscript follows the same basic scene order as the English original, but there are great differences in content.[49]

In 1620 the first German edition of the play appears in a collection, <u>Engelische Comedien und Tragedien</u>.[50] There has been a great deal of speculation as to the origin of this edition,[51] but all scholars agree that it is quite different from the English original and even from the 1608 manuscript. Albert Cohn concludes that for the entire collection we have "nothing but the subjects of the pieces which had been brought over by the English players, not the pieces themselves

---

[48] The title page of the 1606 quarto presents the play "as it hath been acted by the Queens Majesties Servants." This company had formerly been the Earl of Worcester's men.

[49] Unfortunately, however, all copies of Kramer's unpublished dissertation have been lost, and until one can be found we have only his abstract as evidence of his conclusions.

[50] One copy of this collection is the library of the University of Munich. See Kramer, <u>Dissertation Abstracts</u>, p. 63.

[51] These arguments are conveniently summarized by L. M. Price, <u>English Literature in Germany</u>, The University of California Publications in Modern Philology, 37 (Berkeley: University of California Press, 1953), 19-20.

in the form in which they were played."[52] Kramer is unwilling to accept Cohn's conclusions, but he does admit that the 1620 edition "is greatly inferior to the earlier German version, and many scenes are no longer in their original position, while still others have been discarded and new ones added."[53] Interestingly, Johannes Bolte, the 1894 editor of the 1620 German play, notes that the later edition greatly reduces the historical matter of the original while expanding the comic scenes with the characters Nobody and Somebody.[54]

In accord with this evidence, the conclusions drawn by Gustaf Freden concerning the composition of the German play seem accurate.[55] Freden argues that Frederick

[52] Cohn, p. cv.

[53] Kramer, Dissertation Abstracts, p. 69.

[54] "Niemand und Jemand, Ein Englisches Drama aus Shakespeare's zeit, ubersetzt von Ludwig Tieck, Herausgegehen von Johannes Bolte," ShJ, 29-30 (1894), 4-36. L. M. Price notes that in the English original about one third of the play is comedy, while in the 1608 version the proportion rises to half, and in the 1620 edition to two thirds--The Reception of English Literature in Germany, p. 20.

[55] Gustaf Freden, "A Propos Du Theatre Anglais En Allemagne: L'Auteur Inconnu Des Comedies Et Tragedies Anglaises De 1620," Revue De Litterature Comparee, VIII (1928), 420-432. Freden's position is summarized by Price, English Literature in Germany, pp. 20-21.

Menius, who claimed to be the author of the collection of plays,[56] actually had attended the plays and had reconstructed them from notes and memory. As evidence that the version was not based on an existing manuscript or promptbook, Freden cites the presence of traditional German stage directions rather than more contemporary German translations of English terms, the inconsistency of speech-headings, literary stage directions, and inappropriate jumps in action. Freden's logical conclusion then is that the play must have been a memorial reconstruction. Kramer adds that his comparison of the 1620 edition and the 1624 edition (a second edition, based on the 1620 text) with the 1608 version, makes it quite clear that the later text "is the MS version after twelve years of degeneration."[57]

Hence, all evidence seems to suggest that neither the 1608 manuscript nor the 1620 edition is of substantive value. The 1620 edition is far removed from the

[56] This was first noted by Johan Nordstrom in 1922, as cited by Price, English Literature in Germany, p. 20.

[57] Kramer, Dissertation Abstracts, p. 70. He also argues that Green or some member of his troupe is responsible for the 1620 edition. Even if this is true, however, the disintegration of the text noted by Freden is still present, and hence the value of the edition is not increased.

English original, is greatly changed in action, is in prose and not verse, and is probably based on a memorial reconstruction of an acted version of the 1608 manuscript. There is no evidence suggesting that it is based on the English original. The 1608 manuscript is certainly closer to the original than the 1620 edition, but it too is a memorial reconstruction. Regardless of the fact that it roughly follows the senario of the original, scholars have found no evidence to show that it has been directly influenced by either the author, a manuscript, a promptbook, or a copy of the 1606 edition. The only substantive text then on which a modern edition can be based is the 1606 quarto edition.

There is no external evidence on which to determine the printer's copy for this quarto, but what internal evidence there is points rather conclusively to the use of the author's foul papers or perhaps to a fair copy made with great fidelity to the foul papers.[58] F. J. Kramer was accurate in calling the 1606 edition a "good" quarto in that "it meets all the requirements which Mr. A. W. Pollard has set up," but he then concludes that

---

[58] I mention this possibility because of the persuasive argument set forth by Fredson Bowers in <u>On Editing Shakespeare</u> (Charlottesville: The University Press of Virginia, 1966), pp. 20-22. I find no evidence in the quarto that precludes the use of such a fair copy, or that requires the use of foul papers.

it "is clearly an authentic edition, based upon the actor's copy--the 'play book'."[59] On the contrary, there is little evidence that points to the use of prompt copy, and some rather convincing evidence to support the use of foul papers.[60]

W. W. Greg notes that perhaps the strongest evidence that points to the use of foul papers for printer's copy lies "in indefinite directions and in what may be called permissive or petitory [sic.] directions."[61] There are six such directions in the quarto: "<u>Enter</u> Somebody <u>with two or three servants</u>" (ll. 302.1-.2), "<u>Enter three or four</u>" (l. 830.1), "<u>Enter</u> Somebody <u>with two or three</u>" (l. 855.1), "<u>Enter</u> Archigallo . . . <u>and others</u>" (ll. 1081.1-.2), "<u>Enter</u> Elidure <u>crowned, all the lords and ladies, attendants</u>" (ll. 1144.1-.2), and "<u>Enter</u> Somebody <u>and officers</u>" (l. 1613.1).

R. B. McKerrow calls attention to the confusion that would arise in a prompt book from irregular character designations, and posits that such irregularities point away from prompt copy and to the author's foul

---

[59]F. J. Kramer, Dissertation Abstracts, p. 65.

[60]The criteria used for determining these categories are established by W. W. Greg, The Shakespeare First Folio (Oxford: The Clarendon Press, 1955), pp. 105-74, and Fredson Bowers, pp. 10-66.

[61]Greg, p. 135.

papers.[62] There are several instances of such irregularity in the 1606 quarto. In the stage directions Lord Sicophant is usually referred to as "Sicophant," but once he is called "Flatterer" (1. 1023.1). Archigallo is normally referred to by name, but once he is called simply "King" (1. 267.1). Given the large number of characters who are designated functionally in the play (i.e., Prentice, Constable, Braggart) it is not improbable that the author thought of Sicophant in terms of his functional role at this point in the play, but it is unlikely that such a difference would remain in a prompt copy. The same is true of the title "King," especially considering the many shifts of position that exist in the play.

Similarly, in the speech headings two characters are referred to by the same name, "Clown." (They are the country bumpkin, 1. 104.1, and the servant to Nobody, 1. 376.1). Possibly the author was thinking of this role for one particular member of the company who played the clown or comic servant roles, but in any event such designation would probably be too confusing to be retained in a promptbook. In the same way character

[62]R. B. McKerrow, "A Suggestion Regarding Shakespeare's Manuscripts," RES, 11 (1935), 459-65.

designations such as "1 Man" and "2 Man" (ll. 519-20) and "1", "2", and "3" (ll. 837-44) could be very confusing to a prompter, and point more towards an author's general conception of a scene rather than to a prompter's need to know specifically who is on stage. Abbreviated speech prefixes such as "C" (l. 1552) and "Q" (l. 1694) would also probably be regularized in a prompt copy, and point to the rapidity with which an author might work rather than to the specific accuracy needed by a prompter.[63]

Although stage directions cannot be taken as conclusive evidence of either foul papers or prompt copy, seven of the thirteen categories established by Greg as indicative of author's stage directions are represented in the quarto:[64] the status and relationship of characters is defined (<u>Enter a man meeting his wife</u>, ll. 487.1), the grouping of characters on stage is noted (<u>Alarum, they watch the doors. Enter at one door</u> Cornwell, ll. 1370.1-.2), required props are cited (<u>Enter . . . with drum and colors</u>, ll. 1629.1-.2), action accompanying or following an entrance is described (<u>Alarum, excursions; Peridure and Vigenius fight, and</u>

---

[63] In line 1377.1 the entrance of Lady Elidure is marked simply by "Enter Elidure"; at first glance this might be taken as an example of irregular character designation, but it is more likely a compositor's error.

[64] Greg, pp. 124-32.

both slain, ll. 1671.1-.2), independent action is marked (They wrestle and are parted, 1. 1538.1), characters are described on entrance (Enter in state . . . , 1. 1785.1), and noises are called for off-stage (A noise within: Follow, follow, follow, 1. 854.1). These examples are not conclusive of anything in and of themselves, but when combined with the other evidence cited, they tend to weight the case in favor of the use of foul papers or a fair copy faithful to them.

In addition, Greg notes that duplications or tangles in the text may indicate revisions or cancellations that the author intended but never accomplished, and hence may be evidence of foul papers.[65] There are two such instances in the play. At line 376 Somebody has just finished his plans to discredit Nobody in the country, when Nobody enters. Somebody says he will now listen to see if his plan has worked, and we find that it has. Clearly not enough time has elapsed for the actions of the servant to have been effective. Either the author was working with double time much as Shakespeare does in Othello and was not concerned with this inconsistency, or he meant the contrast to be comic, or he meant to revise the passage to make it consistent but

---

[65] Ibid., pp. 110-11.

did not. No definite conclusion can be drawn, but the inconsistency does exist.

Similarly, the Queen in ll. 1719-20 refers to Peridure as King and to the death of Vigenius, presumably by Peridure's hand, since she claims the death will make Peridure "odious/Unto his subjects." But there does not seem to be any reason at this point for assuming that peridure will kill or has killed Vigenius. Sicophant knows that both are dead, but he reveals this fact somewhat later (ll. 1766-67). Why the Queen draws this conclusion is not clear, and it may be an inconsistency that the author meant to cancel, or a line of development he once pursued or meant to pursue further, but abandoned and failed to cancel from his foul papers.

As a last argument for foul papers being used as prompt copy, Kenneth Muir examined the second Folger copy of the play and discovered that there are marginal notes on leaves A and B that indicate a prompt copy.[66] He concluded that this particular copy was being prepared as a promptbook when it was decided not to produce the play; hence the prompter stopped his work at leaf B and we have a partially prepared promptbook. Although

[66] Kenneth Muir, "An unfinished prompt-book," *SQ*, 9 (1958), 420-22.

the argument is tenuous, this might indicate that a prompt copy was not available, and thus increases the possibility that the printer was working from foul papers or a fair copy of them.

On the other hand there are only three bits of evidence that might point to a promptbook being used as the printer's copy.[67] In lines 179-.1 the stage direction is repeated (Exeunt all but the lords. Manent Cornwell and Martianus), and one might interpret the first general direction as the author's, and the second specific one as the prompter's. However, this is the only instance of such repetition in the play, and it is possible that the second direction was an afterthought of the author and that he meant to cancel the first and did not.

There are also two stage directions in the play that might possibly be considered examples of early entrance designations (ll. 487.1, 1797.1). But neither of them is far enough out of place to be positively identified as belonging to a prompter's hand, and Greg speaks of "the persistent placing of directions a few lines too early" as indicative of prompt copy, a requirement that two examples cannot satisfy.

[67] Again the categories are established by Greg, pp. 138-40.

Hence no strong evidence exists to indicate that a promptbook was used as the printer's copy, and the accumulation of consistent and substantial evidence points to the author's foul papers or a faithful fair copy of them as the printer's copy for the 1606 quarto.

Following the 1606 printing, then, the play was not printed again until 1877 when Alexander Smith published a limited edition of fifty copies for private subscribers. He describes his edition this way: "As nearly as possible, a typographical facsimilie [sic] --page for page, and line for line, with the peculiarities of type and spelling carefully preserved."[68] In 1878 Richard Simpson published the work in his collection The School of Shakespeare, and in 1911 J. S. Farmer published a facsimile edition of the English original.[69] The most recent edition of the three versions of the play is F. J. Kramer's unpublished dissertation done at Ohio State University in 1935. Hence there is no modern edition of the play, the play is somewhat difficult to obtain, and it has never been edited in modern

---

[68] Alexander Smith, Nobody and Somebody (Glasgow: R. Anderson, 1877).

[69] Nobody and Somebody, ed. J. S. Farmer (London: The Tudor Facsimile Texts, 1911).

spelling. In addition no existing edition provides textual notes or glosses of obscure words or phrases, and no existing edition reflects the editorial practices suggested by modern editors like R. B. McKerrow, W. W. Greg, and Fredson Bowers. This edition is designed to fill that void.

Date

Richard Simpson, who was unaware of the play's entry into the Stationer's Register in 1606, set the publication date as some time after 1603, and was the first to conjecture that the play was written in about 1592.[70] He based this conclusion on two observations. (1) The play is similar "in construction and intention" to A Merry Knack to Know a Knave, a play revived in 1592 by Lord Strange's company, and imitated by Henslowe's company with A Knack to Know an Honest Man; because of the similarity of these two plays, Simpson argued that a third company commissioned and performed a similar play, Nobody and Somebody. (2) There is a reference in Nobody and Somebody (ll. 796-98) to the collections for the rebuilding of St. Paul's steeple, which was burned in 1561, and to the apparent mishandling of the funds which

---

[70] Simpson, p. 272.

were received; Simpson notes that controversy over this matter was particularly intense around 1592, and hence the reference in the play provides perhaps "the only hopeful note of date in the play." He further noted the similarity between the character Sicophant and Lord Cobham,[71] as Sicophant was a term Essex frequently used to describe Cobham, and conjectured that ll. 431-464 probably alluded "to Cobham's appointment in 1596 to the Wardenship of the Cinque Ports."[72]

He also argued, however, that even though the play was first written early in the 1590's, and perhaps revised later in the decade, it underwent still a later revision after 1603 into the form now extant.[73] His bases for this claim were (1) the reference in the imprint to the play's having been "acted by the Queens Majesties Servants," and (2) the allusion to James's mass knighting of gentlemen who could afford the honor (ll. 345-48).

Several other scholars have accepted Simpson's conclusions, albeit with some modifications. Johannes Bolte cites all of Simpson's evidence for the composition date of 1592, and only modifies the publication date to 1606 on the basis of the Stationer's Register entry.[74]

[71] Ibid., p. 274. [72] Ibid. [73] Ibid., pp. 272-73.

[74] "Niemand und Jemand . . . von Johannes Bolte," ShJ, 29-30 (1894).

F. J. Kramer draws the same conclusions, adding nothing new to the problem of date. W. W. Greg, however, suggested that Henslowe's reference in his diary to a play *Albre Gallus* written by Heywood and Smith in 1602 might be a corruption of Archigallo, and hence a reference to *Nobody and Somebody*,[75] a theory also set forth by Frederick Fleay[76] and Alfred Harbage.[77]

As scholars have agreed, however, all of the evidence is quite tenuous. Chambers agrees that there was some sort of scandal over the repairing of the steeple of St. Paul's in 1592, but he adds that "the steeple was still unbuilt in James' reign,"[78] a fact that could date the reference as late as 1606. Chambers also argues that if Sicophant is meant to reflect the character of Cobham, the play "must be later than Cobham's disgrace in 1603."[79] *Nobody and Somebody* is similar to *A Merry Knack to Know a Knave*, but the similarity is in no way so far-reaching as to establish a specific relationship

[75] Philip Henslowe, *Henslowe's Diary*, ed. W. W. Greg (London: A. H. Bullen, 1904-1908), II, 230.

[76] Frederick Gard Fleay, *A Biographical Chronicle of the English Drama, 1599-1642* (London: Reeves and Turner, 1891), I, 293-94.

[77] Alfred B. Harbage, *Annals of English Drama, 975-1700*, rev. by Samuel Schoenbaum (London: Methuen, 1964).

[78] Chambers, p. 37.

[79] Ibid.

between them, and while Greg's conjecture about <u>Albre Gallus</u> is ingenious and possible, it was of course set forth only within the realm of possibility.

There is therefore no firm evidence that <u>Nobody and Somebody</u> existed in an edition earlier than 1606. We can assume that the author had read Holinshed,[80] and this allows us to establish 1577 as the terminus a quo. The evidence cited by Simpson seems to suggest a composition of at least one version of the play in the first half of the 1590's, but there is good evidence to support a later revision. Given the regularity of the play's entry into the Stationer's Register, 1606 can be established as the terminus ad quem. Beyond this there is no new evidence on which to base any more precise conclusions.

Authorship

Evidence pertaining to the authorship of <u>Nobody and Somebody</u> is scanty. No author's name appears on the 1606 quarto or in the Stationer's Register entry, and as F. J. Kramer notes, "in attempting to answer the question of authorship, the investigation enters the realm of hypothesis, since it must rely solely upon internal

---

[80] See my introduction, pp. 29-30.

evidence."[81] The name most commonly mentioned in relation to the play is that of Thomas Heywood. Fleay first suggested Heywood's connection with Nobody and Somebody through his theory about the play Albre Gallus (see above, p. 65). Fleay's strongest argument for Heywood's authorship, however, is "the spelling "ey" (for ay or I), which is, as far as my knowledge extends, peculiar to him."[82] Nevertheless, standard works such as the Cambridge Bibliography of English Literature, and critics such as A. M. Clark[83] and S. A. Tannenbaum[84] associate Heywood's name with the play.

Richard Simpson does not deal with the authorship problem, and neither does Irving Ribner, who has written the most extensive modern commentary on the play. The only other conjecture as to authorship is that of F. J. Kramer, who suggests that the play is the last work of Robert Greene, written just before his death in 1592.[85]

[81] Kramer, Dissertation Abstracts, p. 66.

[82] Fleay, pp. 293-94.

[83] A. M. Clark, Thomas Heywood: Playwright and Miscellanist.

[84] S. A. Tannenbaum, John Heywood: A Concise Bibliography (New York: S. A. Tannenbaum, 1946-47).

[85] Kramer, Dissertation Abstracts, pp. 66-67.

His theory is based entirely on the conjectured composition date of 1592, and upon internal evidence. He finds verbal parallels with *George a Greene*, *James IV*, and *Friar Bacon and Friar Bungay*, and metrical patterns "identical to those of *James IV*." He also cites the clear didacticism and directness, the neat use of a double plot, and the "pseudo-chronicle" elements of the play as indicative or characteristic of Greene, and concludes that he wrote the play in imitation of *A Merry Knack to Know a Knave* in an attempt to profit from the play's popularity.

This study, however, has not uncovered any new evidence to support or refute the theories already set forth. The link between *Albre Gallus* and *Nobody and Somebody* seems tenuous at best, and due to the loss of Kramer's work (see note 49), very little can be said about the reliability of his conjectures concerning Greene. The question of authorship then is still an open one, and the writer of *Nobody and Somebody*, like the writer of *Woodstock*, remains in A. P. Rossiter's words "a quiet ghost among that great majority who must for all the troublings of their lives and labours rest ANON."[86]

---

[86] *Woodstock, A Moral History*, ed. A. P. Rossiter (London: Chatto and Windus, 1946), p. 76.

69

Preface

This edition presents a critical, modern-spelling text of <u>Nobody and Somebody</u> for advanced students of Renaissance and Jacobean drama. I have attempted to follow the editorial practices established by such scholars as R. B. McKerrow, W. W. Greg, and Fredson Bowers, and I have used Daniel Seltzer's edition of <u>Friar Bacon and Friar Bungay</u> as a general model for the form of my edition. The text is based on the Harvard Library copy of the 1606 quarto, and I have collated that copy with the first of the two copies of the quarto in the Folger Library, and with those in the Huntington Library and the University of Illinois Library to check press variants. I have also collated my base text with Richard Simpson's edition of the play in <u>The School of Shakespeare</u>, which was based on the British Museum copy of the quarto. The few press variants that exist in these four quarto copies have been cited in the textual notes on the page, and all substantive variants (those which alter essential meaning) between the base text and Simpson are also cited there. In addition, those substantive emendations which I have made in the text are noted at the foot of the page and are asterisked, to direct the reader's attention to a discussion of those emendations in appendix A following the text. Accidental variants are cited in the notes only when they could have substantive meaning. The explanatory notes which appear below the textual notes on each page are designed to gloss obsolete words, or words used in a unique sense, and obscure phrases or references.

I have modernized the spelling of the first quarto as completely as possible. I have retained archaic or variant spellings only where a change would alter the meter or syllabic count of a line, where it would cause the loss of a rhyme, or where retention is necessary to preserve an older meaning of a word. I have expanded all preterite endings which were elided in the copy text, and all elided words, except where such expansion would change the number of syllables in a poetic line or alter an intended dialectical distinction. I have not used the grave accent to indicate syllabic value in a preterite ending, due to the frequent irregularity of the verse.

I have silently altered punctuation to conform with modern practices, except where such alteration causes substantive variation; in those cases the changes are cited in the textual notes. My purpose has been to present a readable text and to prevent any misunderstanding or confusion that the original punctuation might cause for a modern reader. I have expanded all contracted forms of characters' names silently. Editorial stage directions are enclosed in square brackets. I have written out all speech headings fully and have regularized them in accordance with modern editorial practice.

I have numbered the lines of the play consecutively, beginning with the first line of the text, exclusive of the prologue. I have corrected mislineation in the text, and these corrections are recorded in the textual notes, as are all substantive reductions of false verse to prose or lineations of false prose as verse. No attempt has been made to create a metrical regularity that did not seem intended by the author. Two half lines of poetry printed on separate lines in the quarto are here treated as one line, and this alteration is done silently. Since there are no act or scene divisions in the quarto, and since the basic unit of composition or structure in the play is the scene (see above, pp. 23-24), I have adopted the standard practice of dividing the play into consecutively numbered scenes at the points where the stage is cleared. I have also adopted the method first used in the Revels editions of numbering stage directions decimally according to the line of text at which they begin. The first line of a stage direction starting at line 225 is, hence, numbered 225.1, the second line 225.2, and so on.

NO-BODY

and

SOME-BODY.

With the true Chronicle Historie of Elydure,
who was fortunately three severall times
crowned King of England.

The true Coppy thereof, as it hath beene acted by the
Queens Majesties Servants.

Printed for John Trundle and are to be sold at his
shop in Barbican, at the signe of No-body.

The Prologue

A subject, of no subject, we present,
For Nobody is nothing.
Who of nothing can something make?
It is a work beyond the power of wit,
And yet invention is ripe.   5
A moral meaning you must then expect,
Grounded on lesser than a shadow's shadow,
Promising nothing where there wants a tongue,
And deeds as few, be done by Nobody.
Yet something out of nothing we will show,   10
To gain your loves, to whom ourselves we owe.

---

5. ripe] Q1; rife Simpson.

---

    7. lesser . . . shadow] i.e. Nobody.
    8-9. the subject of these clauses is a shadow's shadow.

NOBODY AND SOMEBODY

[i]   <u>Enter</u> Cornwell <u>and</u> Martianus.

CORNWELL.

   My Lord Martianus.

MARTIANUS.

   My Lord of Cornwell.

CORNWELL.

   Morrow.

MARTIANUS.

   Morrow.

CORNWELL.

   You are sad, my lord.   5

MARTIANUS.

                    You melancholy.

CORNWELL.

                                            So,

   The state itself mourns in a robe of woe --

MARTIANUS.

   For the decease of Archigallo's vertues.

   I understand you, noble-minded Cornwell.

7. <u>Simpson assigns to</u> Corne.

What generous spirit draws this British air,

But droops at Archigallo's government?   10

CORNWELL.

And reason, Martianus. When the sun

Struggles to be delivered from the wombe

Of an obscure eclipse, doth not the earth

Mourn to behold his shine enveloped?

O Corbonon! When I did close thine eyes   15

I gave release to Britain's miseries.

                <u>Enter</u> Elidure.

MARTIANUS.

Good morrow to Prince Elidure.

ELIDURE.

The same to you, and you. You are sad, my lords.

Your hearts, I think, are frosty, for your blood

Seems crusted in your faces, like the dew   20

In a September morn. How fares the king?

Have you yet bid good morrow to his highness?

CORNWELL.

The king's not stirring yet.

---

   9. <u>generous</u>] gallant, courageous.
  11. <u>And reason</u>] and for good reason.
  13. <u>obscure</u>] dark.
  15. <u>Corbonon</u>] the former king, father to Archigallo, Elidure, Peridure and Vigenius.

Enter Vigenius *and* Peridure [*apart*].

PERIDURE.

　Yonder's old Cornwell. Come, Vigenius,

　We'll have some sport with him.

VIGENIUS.

　　　　　　　　　　Brother, content.　25

PERIDURE.

　Good morrow to you, brother Elidure.

CORNWELL.

　Good morrow to Cornwell.

VIGENIUS.

　　　　　　　　Morrow, old gray-beard.

CORNWELL.

　My beard's not so gray as your wit's green.

VIGENIUS.

　And why so?

PERIDURE.

　We shall ha' you come out now with some reason　30

　that was born in my great-grandsire's time.

CORNWELL.

　Would you would prove as honest princes as

　your great-grandsire was, or half so wise as

*28. wit's] wits Q1.

your elder brother was. There's a couple of

you! 'Sfoot, I am ashamed you should be of the blood royal.
PERIDURE.

And why, father winter?
CORNWELL.

You do not know your state. There's Elidure,

Your elder brother next unto the king;

He plies his book. When shall you see him trace

Lascivious Archigallo through the streets   40

And fight with common hacksters hand to hand,

To wrest from them their goods and dignities?
PERIDURE.

You are too saucy, Cornwell.
VIGENIUS.

       Bridle your spirit.

ELIDURE.

Your words are dangerous, good honest subject,

Old reverent statesman, faithful servitor.   45

Do not traduce the king, he's virtuous.

---

 36. <u>father winter</u>] old man.
 39. <u>trace</u>] to follow the footsteps or traces of.
 41. <u>hacksters</u>] swaggering ruffians, swashbucklers; also prostitutes' bullies.
 43. <u>saucy</u>] impertinent; occasionally with the notion wanton or lascivious.
 46. <u>traduce</u>] to speak evil of, especially maliciously.

Or say he tread somewhat besides the line
Of virtuous government; his regality
Brooks not taxation. King's greatest royalties
Are that their subjects must applaud their deeds   50
As well as bear them. Their prerogatives
Are mural interponents twixt the world
And their proceedings.

CORNWELL.

Well, well, I have served four kings,
And none of all those four but would have ventured   55
Their safeties on old Cornwell's constancy.
But that's all one; now I am called a dotard.
Go to, though now my limbs be stark and stiff,
When Cornwell's dead, Britain I know will want
So strong a prop. Alas, I needs must weep   60
And shed tears in abundance, when I think
How Archigallo wrongs his government.

VIGENIUS.

Nay, now you'll fall into your techy humor.

---

49. taxation] censure, reproof.
51. prerogatives] special privileges
52. mural interponents] walls which interpose.
54. four kings] Kimarus, Elanius, Marindus, Gorbonianus.
58. stark] lacking suppleness.
63. techy] characterized by irritability.

Enter Lord Sicophant.

SICOPHANT.

   My lords, princes I should have said, and after
lords, I am the usher and harbinger unto the king's   65
most excellent person, and his majesty--

VIGENIUS.

   Is forthcoming.

SICOPHANT.

   Or coming forth, hard by or at hand. Will you
put your gestures of attendance on to give his
majesty the *bonjour*?   70

Enter Archigallo *and two lords*, Morgan [*and*] Malgo.

ALL.

   Good morrow to our sovereign Archigallo.

ARCHIGALLO.

   Morrow.

CORNWELL.

   Why do you frown upon your servants, king?
We love you and you ought to favor us.

69. *printed as verse in* Q1.

---

   69. *gesture*] bearing, deportment.

Will you to Council? Here's petitions, 75
Complaints and controversies twixt your subjects,
Appealing all to you.

ARCHIGALLO.

Let's see those papers. A controversy betwixt
the Lord Morgan and the Lord Malgo concerning
their titles to the Southern Island. We know 80
this cause and what their titles be. You
claim it by inheritance.

MORGAN.

My liege, I do.

ARCHIGALLO.

You by the marriage of Lord Morgan's mother,
To whom it was left jointure. 85

MALGO.

True, gracious sovereign.

ARCHIGALLO.

Whose evidence is strongest? To which part
Inclines the censures of our learned judges?

---

80. <u>Southern Island</u>] I have been unable to discover an exact referent for this term. The most likely meaning would seem to be the Isle of Wight.
85. <u>jointure</u>] the holding of property by the husband and wife for life or as a provision for the latter, in the event of her widowhood. Apparently Morgan's father died, and Malgo now claims the land through his marriage to Morgan's mother.
88. <u>censure</u>] a formal judgment or opinion.

MORGAN.
> We come not here to plead before your grace,
> But humbly to entreat your majesty,   90
> Peruse our evidence and censure it
> According to your wisdom.

ARCHIGALLO.
> What I determine then you'll yield unto?

BOTH.
> We will, my sovereign.

ARCHIGALLO.
> Then that Southern Isle
> We take to our protection, and make you,   95
> Lord, governor thereof.

SICOPHANT.
> I humbly thank your highness.

MALGO.
> I hope your majesty--

ARCHIGALLO.
> Reply not. I but take it to myself
> Because I would not have dissention   100
> Betwixt two peers. I love to see you friends,
> And now the island's mine, your quarrel ends.

96. Lord, governor] Lord governor Q1.

---

89. plead] to argue a case formally in a court.

What's next? A poor northern man's humble petition.
Which is the plaintiff?

      Enter Clown, Wench, *and* Rafe.

RAFE.

I, if it please your majesty; I was betrothed to   105
this maid.

ARCHIGALLO.

Is this true, my wench?

WENCH.

'Tis very true, and like your majesty, but this
tempting fellow after that most feloniously
stole my heart away fro' me, carried it   110
into the church, and I, running after him to
get my heart again, was there married
to this other man.

CLOWN.

'Tis very true, and like your majesty. Though
Rafe were once took for a proper man, yet   115
when I came in place it appeared otherwise.
If your highness note his leg and mine, there
is odds, and for a foot, I dare compare. I

---

109. tempting] attractive, and as a tempter.
118. odds] disparity in quality.

have a waist too, and though I say it that
should not say it, there are faces in place   120
of God's making.

ARCHIGALLO.

Thou art a proper fellow, and this wench is
thine by lawful marriage.

CLOWN.

Rafe, you have your answer, you may be gone.
Your only way to save charges is to buy a   125
halfpennyworth of hobnails for your shoes.
Alas, you might have looked into this before.
Go, silly Rafe, go, away, vanish.

ARCHIGALLO.

Is not this lass a pretty, neat, brown wench?

SICOPHANT.

She is, my liege, and mettle I dare warrant.   130

ARCHIGALLO.

Fellow, how long hast thou been married?

120-121. there are faces in place of God's making] there are faces in this place of God's making. Cf. "he is a man of God's making," Tilley, M 162.

125-126. Your only way . . . for your shoes] you have a long walk home, and you need to protect your shoes if you are going to save the cost of repair.

129. neat] trim or smart in apparel.
129. brown] tanned.
130. mettle] spirited, game.

CLOWN.

    I was, as they say, coupled the same day
that my country man Rafe begun the law.
For to tell your majesty the truth, we are
yet both virgins. It did never freeze betwixt   135
us two in a bed, I assure your grace.

ARCHIGALLO.

    Didst never lie with thy wife?

CLOWN.

    Never yet. But now your majesty hath ended
the matter I'll be so bold as take possession.

ARCHIGALLO.

    Hark, my wench, wilt leave these rustic   140
fellows and stay with me?

WENCH.

    What will your highness do with me?

ARCHIGALLO.

    Why I'll make thee a lady.

WENCH.

    And shall I go in fine clothes like a lady?

---

    133. country man] man from the country.
    133. begun the law] started his lawsuit.
    135-36. It did . . . a bed] the meaning of this phrase is obscure. Perhaps the clown means the warmth of our passion has not been cooled or satisfied. Freeze may also mean to stiffen or harden, hence a reference to an erection. However, neither explanation is wholly satisfactory.

ARCHIGALLO.

    Thou shalt.   145

WENCH.

    I'll be a lady then, that's flat. Sweetheart,

    farewell; I must be a lady, so I must.

CLOWN.

    How now, how now? But hear you, sis.

WENCH.

    Away you clown, away.

CLOWN.

    But will your highness rob me of my spouse?   150

ARCHIGALLO.

    What we will, we will. Away with those slaves.

CLOWN.

    Zounds, if ever I take you in Yorkshire for this!

SICOPHANT.

    Away, you slaves!   [Exit Rafe and Clown.]

CORNWELL.

    My lord, these general wrongs will draw your highness

    Into the common hatred of your subjects.   155

ARCHIGALLO.

    What's that to thee? Old doting lord, forbear.

---

    152. if ever . . . this] probably a threat addressed to Rafe or the wench, meaning I will gain my revenge if I ever lay hold upon you in the country.

What's here? Complaints against one Nobody

For overmuch relieving of the poor,

Helping distressed prisoners, entertaining

Extravagants and vagabonds. What fellow's this?   160

CORNWELL.

My liege, I know him. He's an honest subject

That hates extortion, usury, and such sins

As are too common in this land of Britain.

ARCHIGALLO.

I'll have none such as he within my kingdom.

He shall be banished.   165

SICOPHANT.

Hear my advice, my liege; I know a fellow

That's opposite to Nobody in all things.

As he affects the poor, this other hates them,

Loves usury and extortion. Send him straight

Into the country, and upon my life,   170

Ere many months he will devise some means

To make that Nobody bankrupt, make him fly

His country, and be never heard of more.

ARCHIGALLO.

What dost thou call his name?

---

159. entertaining] maintaining, supporting; taking into one's service.
160. Extravagants] vagrants or wanderers.

SICOPHANT.

    His name is Somebody, my liege. 175

ARCHIGALLO.

    Seek out that Somebody, we'll send him straight.

    What other matters stay to be decided

    Determine you, and you. The rest may follow

    To give attendance.

                      <u>Exeunt all but the</u> Lords [Cornwell

                        <u>and</u> Martianus].

MARTIANUS.

    All's nought already, yet these unripe ills 180

    Have not their full growth, and their next degree

    Must needs be worse than nought, and by what name

    Do you call that?

CORNWELL.

                I know none bad enough:

    Base, vild, notorious, ugly, monstrous, slavish,

    Intolerable, abhorred, damnable; 185

    'Tis worse than bad. I'll be no longer vassal

    To such a tyrannous rule, nor accessory

    To the base sufferance of such outrages.

179.1 Q1 <u>prints two stage directions</u>, Exeunt all but the Lords, <u>and</u> Manent Cornwell and Martianus.

---

    184. <u>vild</u>] vile. Also a form of wild, but not so used here.
    188. <u>sufferance</u>] toleration.

MARTIANUS.

You'll not endure it! How can you remedy

A maim so dangerous and incurable?

CORNWELL.

There is a way; but walls have ears and eyes.

Your ear, my lord, and counsel.

MARTIANUS.

                                        I have ears

Open to such discourse, and counsel apt;

And to the full recovery of these wounds

Made in the sick state, most effectual,   195

A word in private.   [they withdraw].

    Enter Peridure and Vigenius [unseen].

PERIDURE.

Come brother, I am tired with reveling.

My last coranto made me almost breathless.

Doth not the king's last wench foot it with art?

---

   190. maim] the mutilation or loss of some essential part. Here a reference to the body politic.
   190. dangerous] hateful, injurious; also difficult to deal with.
   191. walls have ears and eyes] see Tilley, W 19.
   193. and counsel apt] and I have counsel apt.
   195. effectual] actual, now existing.
   198. coranto] courante. A dance characterized by a running or gliding step.
   199. foot it] to dance.

VIGENIUS.
>Oh rarely, rarely, and beyond opinion. 200
>I like this state, where all are libertines
>But my ambition's pleasure and large will.
>See, see, two of our strict-lived counsellors
>In secret conference. They cannot endure
>This freedom. 205

PERIDURE.
>   Nor the rule of Archigallo,
>Because 'tis subject to his liberty.
>Are they not plotting now for some installment
>And change of state? Old gallants, if you be
>'Twill cost your heads.

VIGENIUS.
>   Bodies and all for me.
>List them; such strict reprovers should not live, 210
>Their austere censures on their kings to give.

CORNWELL.
>He must be, then, deposed.

PERIDURE.
>Ay, are you there? That word sounds treason.

212. be, then, be then Q1; then be Simpson.

---

202. <u>large</u>] lax, free.
210. <u>reprovers</u>] those who condemn, rebuke, and chide.

VIGENIUS.

    Nay, but farther hear.

MARTIANUS.

    The king deposed! How must it be effected?   215

    What strengths and powers can suddenly be levied?

    Who will assist this business to reduce

    The state to better form and government?

VIGENIUS.

    Ay marry, more of that!

CORNWELL.

    All Cornwall's at my beck; Devonshire, our neighbor, 220

    Is one with us; you in the North command.

    The oppressed, wronged, dejected and suppressed

    Will flock on all sides to this innovation.

    The clergy late despised, the nobles scorned,

    The commons trod on, and the law contemned   225

    Will lend a mutual and combined power

    Unto this happy change.

PERIDURE.

    Oh monstrous treason!

*220. Cornwall's] Cornwell's Q1.

---

    223. innovation] a political revolution.
    225. contemned] despised.

MARTIANUS [seeing the brothers, aside to Cornwell].

    My lord, we are betrayed and overheard

    By the two princes!   230

CORNWELL [aside].

    How, betrayed!

MARTIANUS [aside].

    Our plot's discovered.

CORNWELL [aside].

    I'll help it all; do you but sooth me up.

    We'll catch them in the trap they lay for us.

MARTIANUS [aside].

    I'll do't.   235

CORNWELL.

    Now sir, the king deposed,

    Who shall succeed?

MARTIANUS.

    Some would say Elidure.

CORNWELL.

    Tush, he's too mild to rule.

    But there are two young princes, hopeful youths,   240

    And of rare expectation in the land.

    Oh, would they deign to bear this weighty charge

---

    233.   sooth me up] support my statements.
    240.   hopeful] inspiring hope.
    242.   deign] to condescend to accept.

Betwixt them, and support the regal scepter
With joint assistance, all our hopes were full.
VIGENIUS.
A scepter! 245
PERIDURE.
And a crown!
MARTIANUS.
What if we made the motion? We have wills
To effect it; we have power to compass it.
VIGENIUS.
And if I make refusal, heaven refuse me.
PERIDURE.
These counsellors are wise, and see in us 250
More vertue than we in ourselves discern.
Would it were come to such election.
CORNWELL.
My honored lord, we'll break it to those princes,
Those hopeful youths, at our convenient leisure.
MARTIANUS.
With all my heart.

247. made Q1; make Simpson.

---

254. convenient] appropriate.

CORNWELL [aside as they are leaving].

                You that our footsteps watched   255

Shall in the depth of your own wiles be catched.

                  Exeunt [Cornwell and Martianus].

VIGENIUS [coming forward].

  A king!

PERIDURE.

           And wear a crown, a crown imperial!

VIGENIUS.

  And sit in state.

PERIDURE.

                Command.

VIGENIUS.

                    And be obeyed.

PERIDURE.

  Our nobles kneeling.

VIGENIUS.

  Servants homaging and crying Ave.   260

PERIDURE.

  Oh brother, shall we through nice folly

  Despise the proffered bounty of these lords?

256. catched] catcht Q1.

---

  260. Ave] hail, welcome.

VIGENIUS.

    Not for the world. I long to sit in state,

    To purse the bounty of our gracious fate.

PERIDURE.

    To entertain foreign ambassadors.   265

VIGENIUS.

    And have our names ranked in the course of kings.

PERIDURE.

    Shadow us, state, with thy majestic wings.

        <u>Enter</u> [<u>behind</u>] King [Archigallo], Cornwell,

              Martianus, <u>and</u> Elidure.

VIGENIUS.

    Now sir, my brother Archigall deposed--

CORNWELL.

    Deposed! Did you hear that my lord?

VIGENIUS.

    For his licentious rule and such abuses   270

    As we'll pretend 'gainst him in parliament--

ARCHIGALLO.

    Oh monstrous brothers!

---

    264. <u>purse</u>] to put into one's purse.
    266. <u>course of kings</u>] classified in the historical progression of kings.
    267. <u>Shadow</u>] to wrap, enfold.

ELIDURE.

          Oh ambitious youths!

VIGENIUS.

  Thus we'll divide the land: all beyond Trent

  And Humber shall suffice one moiety;

  The south part of the land shall make the tother,   275

  Where we will keep two courts, and reign divided,

  Yet as dear loving brothers.

ARCHIGALLO.

          As vild traitors.

PERIDURE.

  Then, Archigall, thou that hast sat in pomp

  And seen me vassal, shalt behold me crowned,

  Whilst thou with humble knees vailst to my state.   280

ARCHIGALLO [coming forward].

  And when must this be done? When shall my crown

  Be parted and divided into halves?

  You reign on this side Humber, you beyond

  The river Trent: when do you take your states,

---

    273. Trent] a river in central England flowing from Staffordshire, through Derbyshire, and into Lincolnshire where it unites with the river Ouse to form the river Humber.

    274. Humber] an estuary in east England, lying between Yorkshire on the north and Lincolnshire on the south.

    274. moiety] half.

    280. vailst] to bow or bend down to the ground in obeisance.

Sit crowned and sceptered to receive our homage, 285
Our duty, and our humble vassalage?

PERIDURE.

I know not when.

ARCHIGALLO.

Nor you?

VIGENIUS.

Nor I.

ARCHIGALLO.

But I know when you shall repent your pride,
Nor will we use delays in our revenge.
Ambitious boys, we doom you prisonment. 290
Your palace royal shall a jail be made,
Your thrones a dungeon, and your scepters irons
In which we'll bound your proud aspiring thoughts.
Away with them; we will not mount our chair
Till their best hopes be changed to black despair. 295

PERIDURE.

Hear us excuse ourselves!

VIGENIUS.

Or let's discover
Who drew us to this hope of sovereignty.

---

290. boys] a term of contempt.
290. doom you prisonment] doom you to imprisonment.

ARCHIGALLO.

    That shall our further leisures arbitrate;

    Our ears are deaf to all excusive pleas.

    Come unambitious brother Elidure,   300

    Help us to lavish our abundant treasures

    In masques, sports, revels, riots, and strange pleasures.

                             Exeunt [omnes].

[ii] Enter Somebody with two or three servants.

SOMEBODY.

    But is it true the fame of Nobody

    For virtue, almsdeeds, and for charity

    Is so renowned and famous in the country?   305

SERVANT [1].

    Oh lord, sir, ay, he's talked of far and near,

    Fills all the boundless country with applause.

    There lives not in all Britain one so spoke of

    For pity, good mind, and true charity.

SOMEBODY.

    Which Somebody shall alter ere't be long.   310

*302.   masques] masks Q1.

---

   302.   riots] debauchery, unrestrained mirth, noise.
   302.   strange] exceptionally great in degree or amount.

SERVANT [2].

    You may, my lord, being in grace at court

    And the high favors of King Archigallo,

    Exile this petty fellow from the land

    That so obscures the beauty of your deeds.

SOMEBODY.

    What doth this Nobody?

SERVANT [3].

                You shall hear, my lord.   315

    Come twenty poor men to his gate at once;

    Nobody gives them money, meat and drink,

    If they be naked, clothes. Then come poor soldiers,

    Sick, maimed, and shot, from any foreign wars;

    Nobody takes them in, provides them harbor,   320

    Maintains their ruined fortunes at his charge.

    He gives to orphans, and for widows builds

    Almshouses, spittles, and large hospitals;

    And when it comes in question who is apt

    311-12. being . . . Archigallo] the sense of "in grace" carries over to mean "and in the high favors of King Archigallo."

    313. petty] minor, inferior.

    321. maintains . . . fortunes] provides for the continuence of their fortunes.

    323. spittles] houses or places especially for low persons with foul diseases.

    323. hospitals] charitable insitutions for the housing and maintenance of the needy.

    324. apt] inclined, given to doing.

For such good deeds, 'tis answered Nobody.

Now Nobody hath entertained again

Long - banished hospitality, and at his board

A hundred lusty yeomen daily waits,

Whose long backs bend with weighty chines of beef

And choice of cheer, whose fragments at his gate   330

Suffice the general poor of the whole shire.

Nobody's table's free for travlers,

His buttery and his cellar ope to all

That starve with drought, or thirst upon the way.

SOMEBODY.

His fame is great. How should we help it?   335

SERVANT [3].

My lord, 'tis past my reach. 'Tis you must do it,

Or't must be left undone.

SOMEBODY.

What deeds of note is he else famous for?

---

    328. lusty] healthy, strong.
    329. chine] a joint, consisting of the whole or part of the backbone of an animal, with the adjoining flesh.
    330. choice of cheer] an abundance and variety of food.
    330. fragments] pieces broken off, crumbs. There is so much food, the pieces that break off while the food is being carried in feed all the poor of the shire.
    333. buttery] a place for storing liquor.
    333. cellar] a storeroom for provisions.
    335. help] meant ironically.
    336. reach] range of mind or thought.

SERVANT [1].

    My lord, I'll tell you.

    His barns are full, and when the cormorants   340

    And wealthy farmers hoard up all the grain,

    He empties all his garners to the poor

    Under the stretched price that the market yields.

    Nobody racks no rents, doth not oppress

    His tenants with extortions. When the king   345

    Knighted the lusty gallants of the land,

    Nobody then made dainty to be knighted,

    And indeed kept him in his known estate.

SOMEBODY.

    The slave's ambitious, and his life I hate.

SERVANT [2].

    How shall we bring his name in public scandal?   350

SOMEBODY.

    Thus it shall be, use my direction.

    In court and country I am Somebody,

---

    340. <u>cormorants</u>] insatiably greedy persons.
    343. <u>stretched</u>] enlarged beyond proper limits.
    344. <u>racks no rents</u>] does not raise rents above a fair and normal price.
    345. <u>When . . . land</u>] "This looks like a reference to James' fiscal distribution of the honour," Simpson, p. 18.
    347. <u>made dainty</u>] was chary or loth.
    351. <u>use my direction</u>] follow my instructions.

And therefore apt and fit to be employed.

Go thou in secret, being a subtle knave,

And sow seditious slanders through the land; 355

Oppress the poor, suppress the fatherless,

Deny the widows food, the starved relief;

And when the wretches shall complain their wrongs,

Being called in question, swear 'twas Nobody.

Rack rents; raise prices; 360

Buy up the best and choice commodities

At the best hand, then keep them till their prices

Be lifted to their height, and double rate;

And when the raisers of this dearth are sought,

Though Somebody do this, protest and swear 365

'Twas Nobody 'fore judge and magistrate.

Bring scandals on the rich; raise mutinous lies

Upon the state and rumors in the court;

Backbite and sow dissention amongst friends,

Quarrels mongst neighbors, and debate mongst strangers;

---

358. complain] to make a formal statement of a grievance before a competent authority.

361. commodities] parcels of goods sold on credit by a usurer to a needy person, who immediately raised some cash by reselling them at a lower price, generally to the usurer himself.

362. At the best hand] most profitably or cheaply.

363. double rate] charge twice the normal rate.

369. Backbite] to slander a person absent.

370. debate] strife, dissention.

Set man and wife at odds, kindred at strife;

And when it comes in question, to clear us

Let everyone protest and swear for one,

And so the blame will fall on Nobody.

About it then; if these things well succeed, 375

You shall prevail, and we applaud your speed.

[Exit Servants.]

Enter Nobody and the Clown.

See where he comes. I will withdraw and see

The event and fortunes of our last policy.

[withdraws.]

NOBODY.

Come on mine own servant, some news, some news.

What report have I in the country, how am I 380

talked on in the city, and what fame bear

I in the court?

CLOWN.

Oh master, you are half hanged.

NOBODY.

Hanged! why man?

---

373. swear for one] to answer for someone or for oneself under oath.
376. applaud your speed] reward your success.
376.1 the Clown] not the same character as in line 104.1; perhaps the clown of the company.
378. event] result.

CLOWN.
> Because you have an ill name. A man had almost 385
> serve no master as serve you. I was carried
> afore the constable but yesterday, and they
> took me up for a stravagant. They asked me
> whom I served; I told them Nobody; they
> presently drew me to the post, and there gave 390
> me the law of arms.

NOBODY.
> The law of arms?

CLOWN.
> Ay, as much law as their arms were able to
> lay on; they tickled my collifodium. I rid
> post for a quarter of an hour with switch, 395
> though not with spur.

NOBODY.
> Sure Somebody was the cause of all.

---

    388.   stravagant] a vagrant.
    390.   post] whipping post.
    394.   tickled my collifodidum] tickle means to beat. I cannot discover a referent for collifodium; it may be the clown's malapropism for a scientific term defining a portion of the anatomy, (i.e. buttocks?).
    394-396.   I rid . . . spur] a pun on riding post, conveying a message swiftly, and being switched at the post.

CLOWN.

    I'll be sworn of that. Somebody tickled me

    a heat, and that I felt. But master, why

    do you go thus out of fashion? You are even   400

    a very hoddy-doddy, all breech--

NOBODY.

    And no body. But if my breeches had as much

    cloth in them as ever was drawn betwixt

    Kendal and Canning Street, they were scarce

    great enough to hold all the wrongs that I   405

    must pocket.

    Fie, fie, how I am slandered through the world.

    Nobody keeps tall fellows at his heels,

    Yet if you meet a crew of rogues and beggars,

    Ask who they serve; they'll answer Nobody.   410

    398-99. tickled me a heat] beat me until my skin turned red and hot.
    401. hoddy-doddy] a short, dumpy person.
    401. all breech] all breeches, or all rump.
    404. Kendal and Canning Street] Kendal was a city in Westmoreland, famous for a kind of cloth (Kendal green); Canning Street is probably a reference to Candlewick Street, also known as Cannon Street, and now as Watling Street. In the ballad "London Lyckpeny" the narrator goes through "Canwyke street" where "Drapers mutch cloth me ofred anone." See Stanley Rubinstein, Historians of London (Hamden, Conn.: Archon, 1968), pp. 107-109.
    406. pocket] endure, submit to.
    408. tall] brave, valiant.
    408. at his heels] in close attendance.

>   Your cavaliers and swaggerers bout the town,
>   That domineer in taverns, swear and stare,
>   Urge them upon some terms; they'll turn their malice
>   To me and say they'll fight with Nobody.
>   Or if they fight, and Nobody by chance   415
>   Come in to part them, I am sure to pay for it,
>   And Nobody be hurt when they scape scot-free;
>   And not the dastard'st coward in the world
>   But dares a bout with me. What shall I do?
>
> SOMEBODY [aside].
>   Do what thou wilt, before we end this strife,   420
>   I'll make thee ten times weary of thy life.
>
> CLOWN.
>   But do you hear master, when I have served
>   you a year or two, who shall pay me
>   my wages?
>
> NOBODY.
>   Why Nobody.   425

*419. a bout] Simpson; about Q1.

---

    411. cavaliers] roistering, swaggering fellows.
    411. swaggerers] quarrellers.
    412. domineer] to dominate, to assume lordly airs.
    412. swear and stare] to open the eyes wide in madness or fury.
    413. Urge . . . terms] provoke or challenge them upon some position or circumstance.
    418. dastard'st] most despicable.

CLOWN.

    Indeed, if I serve Nobody, Nobody must pay
me my wages. Therefore I'll even seek out
Somebody or other to get me a new service.
But the best is, master, if you run away
you are easy to be found again.   430

NOBODY.

    Why so sir?

CLOWN.

    Marry, ask a deaf man whom he hears,
he'll straight say Nobody. Ask the blindest
beetle that is whom he sees and he'll
answer Nobody. He that never saw in his   435
life can see you, though you were as little
as a mote, and he that never heard
can hear you, though you tread as softly
as a mouse. Therefore I shall be sure
never to lose you. Besides, you have one   440
commodity, master, which none hath besides
you; if you should love the most fickle and

---

    427. <u>even</u>] just now.
    434. <u>beetle</u>] an intellectually blind person, from the notion that beetles fly right into people's faces; hence blind as a beetle.
    437. <u>mote</u>] a particle of dust.
    441. <u>commodity</u>] advantage.

inconstants wench that is in the world,

she'll be true to Nobody, therefore constant

to you.   445

NOBODY.

And thou sayest true in that, my honest servant.

Besides, I am in great especial grace

With the King, Archigallo, that now reigns

In tyranny and strange misgovernment;

Nobody loves him, and he loves Nobody.   450

But that which most torments my troubled soul,

My name is made mere opposite to virtue.

For he is only held peaceful and quiet

That quarrels, brawls, and fights with Nobody;

He's honest held that lies with Nobody's wife;   455

And he that hurts and injures Nobody,

All the world says, ay, that's a virtuous man.

And though a man have done a thousand mischiefs,

And come to prove the forfeit made to law,

If he can prove he hath wronged Nobody,   460

No man can touch his life. This makes me mad;

This makes me leave the place where I was bred,

---

443. <u>inconstants</u>] most inconstant.
452. <u>mere</u>] the absolute.
459. <u>to prove . . . law</u>] to test or try the loss of rights due to the commission of a crime.
462. <u>place where I was bred</u>] the country.

And thousand times a day to wish me dead.

SOMEBODY [aside]

And I'll pursue thee wheresoe'er thou fliest,

Nor shalt thou rest in England till thous diest. 465

CLOWN.

Master, I would wish you to leave the country and

see what good entertainment you will have

in the city. I do not think but there you

will be most kindly respected. I have been

there in my youth; there's hospitality, and you 470

talk of hospitality; and they talk of you

'bomination to see. For there, master, come to

them as often as you will, four times a day,

and they'll make Nobody drink. They love to

have Nobody trouble them, and without good 475

security they will lend Nobody money.

Come into Birchin Lane, they'll give Nobody a

suit, choose where he list; go into Cheapside, and

---

472. 'bomination] abomination; to an extreme.
477. Birchin Lane] literally a street extending from Cornhill, opposite the east end of the Royal Exchange, to Lombard Street, and famous for ready-made men's apparel. Also used figuratively to mean whipping, thrashing, or birching lane.
478. Cheapside] originally a large open common in the course of Watling Street where the markets and public assemblies were held.

Nobody may take up as much plate as he
can carry. 480

NOBODY.

Then I'll to London, for the country tires me
With exclamations and with open wrongs,
Sith in the city they affect me so.

CLOWN.

O master, there I am sure Nobody may
have anything without money; Nobody may 485
come out of the tavern without paying
his reckoning at his pleasure.

Enter a man meeting his wife.

NOBODY.

That's better than the country. Who comes here?

[*they withdraw.*]

1 MAN.

Minion, where have you been all this night?

WIFE.

Why do you ask, husband? 490

1 MAN.

Because I would know, wife.

---

482. *exclamations*] loud complaints or expressions of anger.

WIFE.

   I have been with Nobody.

NOBODY [aside].

   'Tis a lie, good man! Believe her not, she was not with me.

1 MAN.

   And who hath lain with you tonight?   495

WIFE.

   Lie with me? Why Nobody.

NOBODY [aside].

   Oh monstrous! They would make me a whoremaster.

1 MAN.

   Well, I do not think but Somebody hath been with you.

SOMEBODY [aside].

   Somebody was indeed.   500

WIFE.

   God's life, husband, you do me wrong; I lay with Nobody.

1 MAN.

   Well minion, though Nobody bear the blame,

   Use it no more, lest Somebody bide the shame.

                [Exit wife.]

NOBODY [aside].

   I will endure no longer in this climate.

---

  503. Use] to pursue some course of action. Also, to have sexual intercourse with.

It is so full of slanders, I'll to the city, 505
And there perform the deeds of charity.

Enter the 2 man and a prentice.

2 MAN.

Now you rascal, who have you been withal at the alehouse?

PRENTICE.

Sooth, I was with Nobody.

NOBODY [aside].

Not with me! 510

2 MAN.

And who was drunk there with you?

PRENTICE.

Sooth, Nobody was drunk with me.

NOBODY [aside].

O intolerable! They would make me a drunkard too.
I cannot endure any longer, I must hence;
No patience with such scandals can dispense. 515

2 MAN.

Well sirrah, if I take you so again, I'll so belabor you--O neighbor, good morrow.

---

515. dispense] excuse or condone.
517. belabor] to thrash with all one's might.

1 MAN.

> Good morrow.

2 MAN.

> You are sad methinks.

1 MAN.

> Faith sir, I have cause. I have lent a 520
> friend of mine a hundred pound and have
> Nobody's word for the payment; bill, nor bond,
> nor anything to show.

2 MAN.

> Have you Nobody's word? I'll assure you that
> Nobody is a good man, a good man I assure 525
> you neighbor. Nobody will keep his word;
> Nobody's word is as good as his bond.

1 MAN.

> Ay, say you so? Nay then, let's drink down sorrow;
> If none would lend, then Nobody should borrow.
>
> > [Exit. 1 Man, 2 Man and Prentice.]

NOBODY.

> Yet there's one keeps a good tongue in his head 530
> That can give Nobody a good report;
> I am beholding to him for his praise.

---

522. bill, nor bond] elliptical; I have neither bill (promissory note) nor bond (a deed by which A binds himself to pay a certain sum of money to B).

But since my man so much commends the city,
I'll thither, and to purchase me a name,
Take a large house of infinite receipt,   535
There keep a table for all good spirits,
And all the chimneys shall cast smoke at once.
There I'll give scholars pensions, poets gold,
Arts their deserts, philosophy due praise,
Learning his merit, and all worth his meed   540
There I'll release poor prisoners from their dungeons,
Pay creditors the debts of other men,
And get myself a name mongst citizens,
That aftertimes partakers of all bliss
May thus record, Nobody did all this.   545
Country, farewell, whose slanderous tongues I fly;
The city now shall lift my name on high.   [Exit.]
SOMEBODY.
Whether I'll follow thee with swallow's wings
And nimble expedition, there to raise
New brawls and rumors to eclipse they praise.   550
Those subtle, sly, insinuating fellows
Whom Somebody hath sent into the country

---

534. purchase] win, earn.
535. house] an inn or tavern.
535. receipt] capability of accomodating; capacity.
540. meed] reward, merited portion of honor.
548. with swallow's wings] as swift as the swallow.
549. expedition] haste, speed.
550. brawls] noisy quarrels, clamors.

To rack, transport, extort, and to oppress,
Will I call home, and all their wits employ
Against this public benefactor, known   555
Honest, for all the rumors by us sown.
But howsoever, I am sworn his foe,
And opposite to all his meriting deeds.
This way must do, though my divining thoughts
This augury amidst their changes have,   560
That Somebody will at length be proved a knave.

         Exeunt.

[iii] Enter Queen, Sicophant, and Lady
     Elidure severally.

SICOPHANT.

Good day to you both, fair ladies,
But fairest of them both my gracious queen.
Good day to your high majesty, and madam,
The royal lady of great Elidure,   565

*560. amidst] amidsts Q1.

---

 553. transport] here, to transfer or convey property or goods illegally.
 559. divining] prophesying.
 560. augury] indication of the future.

My sovereign's brother, unto you I wish

This morning prove as gracious and as good.

QUEEN.

Those greetings from the Lady Elidure

Would pleasingly sound in our princely ears.

LADY.

Such greetings from great Archigallo's Queen   570

Would be most gracious to our princely ear.

QUEEN.

What, no good morrow and our grace so near?

Reach me my glove.

LADY.

                Whom speaks this woman to?

QUEEN.

Why to my subject, to my waiting maid.

Am not I mighty Archigallo's Queen?   575

Is not my lord the royal English King,

Thy husband and thyself my servitors?

LADY.

Is my coach ready? Where are all my men

That should attend upon our awful frown?

---

573. "Compare II. Hen. VI., I. iii. 1. 141, where the Queen tells the Duchess of Gloucester to pick up her fan, and gives her a box on the ear--pretending to take her for someone else,"--Simpson.

579. <u>awful</u>] worthy of profound respect or reverential fear.

What, not one near?

QUEEN.

                        Minion, my glove.   580

SICOPHANT.

Madam, her highness' glove.

LADY.

My scarf is fallen, one of you reach it up.

QUEEN.

You hear me?

LADY.

                  Painted majesty, be gone.

I am not to be counterchecked by any.

QUEEN.

Shall I bear this?

SICOPHANT.

                    Be patient, I will school her.   585

Your excellence greatly forgets yourself

To be so dutiless unto the queen.

I have seen the world, I know what 'tis to obey

And to command. What if it please the queen

That you her subject should attend on her   590

And take her glove up; is it meet that I

---

591. <u>meet</u>] fitting.

>   Should stoop for yours? You're proud, fie, fie, you're
>   proud.
>   This must not be twixt such two royal sisters,
>   As you by marriage are; go to, submit,
>   Her majesty is easy to forgive.   595
>
> LADY.
>   Saucy lord, forbear. There's for your exortation.
>   [strikes him.]
>
> QUEEN.
>   I cannot bear this, 'tis insufferable.
>   I'll to the king, and if he save thy life
>   He shall have mine. Madness and wrath attend,
>   My thoughts are leveled at a bloody end.   600
>   [Exit Queen.]
>
> LADY.
>   She's shadow,
>   We the true substance are. Follow her those
>   That to our greatness dare themselves oppose.
>   [Enter Cornwell, Martianus, Morgan and Malgo.]
>
> CORNWELL.
>   Health to your ladyship; I would say queen
>   If I might have my mind, by'r Lady, lady.   605

593. such two] Q1; two such Simpson. 596. strikes him] Simpson.

MARTIANUS.

   I had a suit unto the king with this lord

   For the great office of High Seneschal,

   Because of our good service to the state.

   But he in scorn, as he doth everything,

   Hath tane it from us both, and gin't a fool.   610

MORGAN.

   To a Sicophant, a courtly parasite.

SICOPHANT.

   Bear witness, madam, I'll go tell the king

   That they speak treason.

MALGO.

                Pass upon our swords,

   You old exchequer of all flattery.

   I tell thee Archigallo shall be deposed,   615

   And thou disrobed of all they dignity.

SICOPHANT.

   I hope not so.

CORNWELL.

                See here the council's hands,

   Subscribed to Archigallo's overthrow.

   The names of sixteen royal English peers

---

   607. <u>High Seneschal</u>] an official in the household of a sovereign to whom the administration of justice and entire control of domestic arrangements were entrusted.
   610. <u>gin't</u>] given it.

          Joined in a league that is inviolate,   620

          And nothing wants but Elidurus' grant

          To accept the kingdom when the deed is done.
SICOPHANT.

          Nay then, I'll take your parts and join with you.
MARTIANUS.

          We will not have a clawback's hand commixed

          With such heroic peers.
SICOPHANT.

                              I hope my lady   625

          Is not of their minds. My most gracious queen,

          What I did speak in reprehensive sort

          Was more because her majesty was present

          Than any offense of yours, and so esteem it.

          God knows I love your highness and these lords.   630
LADY.

          Which of you will persuade my Elidure

          To take upon him England's royalty?
MARTIANUS.

          Madam, we all have so importuned him,

          Laying unto his judgement everything

---

     621. <u>wants</u>] is lacking.
     624. <u>clawback</u>] one who claws or strokes another's back;
a flatterer.
     624. <u>commixed</u>] intermixed.
     627. <u>in reprehensive sort</u>] reprehensively.

               That might attract his senses to the crown,   635
               But he, frost-brained, will not be obtained
               To take upon him this realm's government.
MALGO.
               He is the very soul of lenity.
               If ever moderation lived in any,
               Your lord with that rich virtue is possessed.   640
LADY.
               This mildness in him makes me so despised
               By the proud queen and by her favorites.

                         Enter Elidure.

CORNWELL.
               See, madam, where he comes reading a book.
LADY.
               My lord and husband, with your leave, this book
               Is fitter for an university   645
               Than to be looked on, and the crown so near.
               You know these lords for tyranny have sworn
               To banish Archigallo from the throne,
               And to invest you in the royalty;

---

   636. frost-brained] OED cites this usage as meaning dull or stupid, but frost as meaning coldness of behavior or temperament seems closer to Elidure's character.
   638. lenity] mildness, gentleness.

  Will you not thank them, and with bounteous hands   650
  Sprinkle their greatness with the names of earls,
  Dukes, marquesses, and other higher terms?
ELIDURE.
  My dearest love, the essence of my soul,
  And you my honored lords, the suit you make,
  Though it be just for many wrongs imposed,   655
  Yet unto me it seems an injury.
  What is my greatness by my brother's fall,
  But like a starved body nourished
  With the destruction of the other limbs?
  Innumerable are the griefs that wait   660
  On hoarded treasures, then much more on crowns.
  The middle path, the golden mean for me;
  Leave me obedience, take you majesty.
LADY.
  Why this is worser to my lofty mind
  Than the late checks given by the angry queen.   665
CORNWELL.
  If you refuse it, know we are determined
  To lay it elsewhere.

*658. body <u>Simpson conjectures</u> belly.

---

 664. <u>lofty</u>] directed to high objects or position.

LADY.

                On your younger brother,
And then, no doubt, we shall be awed indeed,
When the ambition of the elder's wife
Can scarcely give our patience any bounds.   670
England is sick of pride and tyranny,
And in thy goodness only to be cured.
Thou art called forth amongst a thousand men
To minister this sovereign antidote,
To amend thy brother's cruelty with love,   675
And if thou wilt not from oppression free
Thy native country, thou art vild as he.

ELIDURE.

I had rather stay his leisure to amend.

LADY.

Men, heaven, gods, devils, what power should I invoke
To fashion him anew? Thunder come down!   680
Crown me with ruin, since not with a crown.

CORNWELL.

Long life unto the Kingly Elidure!
Trumpets proclaim it, whether he will or no.

---

    667. <u>your younger brother</u>] Peridure or Vigenius.
    668. <u>awed</u>] controlled or struck with fear.
    670. <u>Can . . . bounds</u>] she is so ambitious that she demands boundless patience from us.
    675. <u>amend</u>] to heal or cure.
    678. <u>stay his leisure</u>] to wait for his will or time.

LADY.

    For that conceit, lords, you have won my heart.

    In his despite let him be straightways crowned,   685

    That I may triumph wilst the trumpets sound.

ELIDURE.

    Carry me to my grave, not to a throne.

LADY.

    Help, lords, to seat him, nay help everyone.

    So should the Majesty of England sit,

    Wilst we in like state do associate him.   690

ELIDURE.

    Never did any less desire to reign

    Than I; heaven knows this greatness is my pain.

LADY.

    Pain me in this sort, great lords, every day;

    'Tis sweet to rule.

ELIDURE.

                "Tis sweeter to obey.

CORNWELL.

    Live King of England long and happily!   695

686. whilst] Q1; while <u>Simpson</u>.

---

    684. <u>conceit</u>] an ingenious expression or notion.
    685. <u>despite</u>] scorn, disdain.
    690. <u>associate</u>] accompany.

As long and happily your highness live.

LADY.

We thank you lords; now call in the deposed.

Him and his proud queen bring unto our sight,

That in her wrongs we may have our delight.

Enter Archigallo *and his* queen, *bound.*

ARCHIGALLO.

Betrayed! ta'en prisoner! and by those that owe   700

To me their duty and allegiance!

My brother the usurper of the crown!

Oh this is monstrous, most insufferable.

ELIDURE.

Good brother, grieve not; 'tis against my will

That I am made a king. Pray take my place;   705

I had rather be your subject than your lord.

LADY.

So had not I. Sit still, my gracious lord,

Whilst I look through this tyrant with a frown.

Minion, reach up my glove.

QUEEN.

                Thinkst thou because

---

708. look through] to penetrate with a look.

Thy husband can dissemble piety, 710
And therein hath deposed my royal lord,
That I am lesser in estate than queen?
No, thine own answer lately given to me
I thus revert: stoop thou, proud queen, for me!

SICOPHANT.

Nay, then as I did lately to her highness, 715
I must admonish you. Dejected lady,
You do forget yourself, and where you are.
Duty is debt, and it is fit, since now
You are a subject, to bear humble thoughts.
Follow my counsel, lady, and submit; 720
Her majesty, no doubt, will pardon it.

QUEEN.

There's for your pains.   [strikes him.]

SICOPHANT.

Which way so ere I go,
I have it here, whether it ebb or flow.

---

*714. revert] Simpson in a note; revet Q1.   *716. Dejected] Simpson; diected Q1.   722. strikes him] Simpson.

---

723. I have . . . flow] the exact meaning of the line is unclear. The general sense is I receive the same treatment whether my fortunes are declining or advancing.

LADY.

That pride of thine shall be thy overthrow.

And thus I sentence them:--

ELIDURE.

                      Leave that to me?   725

LADY.

No, you are too mild; judgement belongs to me.

Thou, Archigallo, for thy tyranny

Forever be excluded from all rule,

And from thy life.

ELIDURE.

          Not from his life, I pray.

LADY.

He unto whom the greatest wrongs are done,   730

Dispatch him quickly.

MORGAN.

              That will I.

MALGO.

                      Or I.

ELIDURE.

And therein, lords, effect my tragedy.

LADY.

Why strike you not? Oh 'tis a dangerous thing

To have a living subject of a king;

Much treason may be wrought, when in his death   735

Our safety is secured.

ELIDURE.

    Banish him rather. Oh sweet, spare his life,

    He is my brother.

ARCHIGALLO.

               Crowned, and pray thy wife?

ELIDURE.

    Oh brother, if you roughly speak, I know

    There is no hope but your sure overthrow.   740

    [to Lady Elidure.]

    Pray be not angry with me for my love.

    To banishment, since it must needs be so;

    His life I give him, whoso'er says no.

LADY.

    What! and his lady's too?

ELIDURE.

              Ay, her's and all.

LADY.

    But I'll not have you banished with the king.   745

    No, minion, no, since you must live, be assured

    I'll make thee meanest of my waiting maids.

QUEEN.

    I scorn thy pride.

ARCHIGALLO.

              Farewell deceiving state,

    Pride-making crown, my dearest wife, farewell;

I have been a tyrant, and I'll be so still.   750

                              Exit.

ELIDURE.

   Alas, my brother.

LADY.

                    Dry up childish tears,

   And to these lords that have invested you

   Give gracious looks and honorable deeds.

ELIDURE.

   Give them my crown, o give them all I have!

   Thy throne I reckon but a glorious grave.   755

LADY.

   Then from myself these dignities receive:

   The island wrested from you I restore;

   See it be given them back, Lord Sicophant.

   The office of High Seneschal bereft you,

   My Lord of Cornwell, to your grace we give.   760

   You, Martianus, be our Treasurer,

   And if we find you faithful, be assured

   You shall not want preferment at our hands.

   Meantime, this office we impose on you;

   Be tutor to this lady, and her pride,   765

755. Thy] Q1; The Simpson.

With your learned principles whereof you are full,

Turn to humility, or vex her soul.

QUEEN.

Torment on torment, tutored by a fool.

SICOPHANT.

Madam, it is her highness' will, be pleased

LADY.

Young Peridurus and Vigenius, lords, 770

Release from prison, and because your king

Is mightily affected unto York,

Thether dismiss the court incontinent.

SICOPHANT.

Shall it be so, my liege?

LADY.

      Are not we king?

His silence says it, and what we ordain, 775

Who dares make question of? This day forever

Through our reign be held a festival,

And triumph, lords, that England is set free

From a vild tyrant and his cruelty.

ELIDURE.

On to our funeral, 'tis no matter where;

I sin I know in suffering pride so near.

       Exeunt [omnes].

---

772. affected] favorably inclined.
773. incontinent] without delay.
781. suffering] allowing to exist, tolerating.

[iv]   Enter Nobody, and the Clown.

NOBODY.

Ahem boy, Nobody is sound yet, for all his

troubles.

CLOWN.

And so is Nobody's man, for all his whipping.

But master, we are now in the city, walled   785

about from slander. There cannot a lie

come in but it must run through brick,

or get the good will of the warders

whose brown bills look blue upon all

passengers.   790

NOBODY.

O this city, if Nobody live to be as old again,

be it spoken in secret, I'll have fenced about

with a wall of brass.

CLOWN.

Of Nobody's making, that will be rare.

NOBODY.

I'll bring the Thames through the middle of it, empty   795

---

    782. sound] healthy.
    788. warders] soldiers set to guard an entrance.
    789. brown bills] halberds, or similar weapons used by the watch.
    789. look blue upon] affect with fear or anxiety.
    790. passengers] travellers.
    793. wall of brass] cf. Friar Bacon and Friar Bungay, xi, 20 (ed. Daniel Seltzer).

Moor Ditch at my own charge, and build up
Paul's steeple without a collection. I see
not what becomes of these collections.
CLOWN.
Why Nobody receives them.
NOBODY.
I, knave?   800
CLOWN.
You knave, or as the world goes, Somebody
receives all, and Nobody is blamed for it.
NOBODY.
But is it rumored so throughout the city?
CLOWN.
Do not you know that? There's not an orphan's
portion lost out of the chamber, but Nobody   805
has got it; no corn transported without
warrant, but Nobody has done it; no goods
stolen but by Nobody; no extortion without Nobody;
and but that truth will come to light, few
wenches got with child, but with Nobody.   810

---

   805. portion] the part or share of an estate given or passing by law to an heir.
   805. chamber] treasury.
   806-07. no corn . . . warrant] "the offences against the protectionist code which forbad all export of raw material, wool, corn, or metal"--Simpson, p. 270.

NOBODY.

Nay, that's by Somebody!

CLOWN.

I think Somebody had a hand in't, but Nobody sometimes pays for the nursing of it.

NOBODY.

Indeed I have taken into my charge many a poor infant left to the alms of the wide world;   815
I have helped many a virtuous maid to a good husband, and ne'er desired her maidenhead; redeemed many gentlemen's lands, that have thanked Nobody for it; built pesthouses and other places of retirement in the sickness time   820
for the good of the city; and yet Nobody cannot get a good word for his labor.

CLOWN.

'Tis a mad world, master.

NOBODY.

Yet this mad world shall not make me mad. I

---

    813. <u>nursing</u>] rearing.
    820. <u>the sickness time</u>] "Years of plague were 1593 and 1603"--Simpson.
    823. <u>'Tis</u> . . . <u>master</u>] cf. Tilley, w880.

              Am all spirit, Nobody. Let them grieve   825
           That scrape for wealth; I will the poor relieve.
           Where are the masters of the several prisons,
           Within and near adjoining to the city,
           That I may spread my charity abroad.
CLOWN.
           Here they be, sir.

                    Enter three or four.
NOBODY.
                             Welcome, gentlemen.   830
           You are they that make poor men householders
           Against their wills, and yet do them no wrong.
           You have the actions and the cases of your sides,
           Whilst your tenants in common want money to fill them.
           How many gentlemen of less revenues than Nobody   835
           Lie in your knight's ward for want of maintenance?

824-25. I/Am all   I am/All Q1.

---

   825. spirit] pun: courage, and the immaterial part of a person.
   826. scrape] gather together money with labor and difficulty.
   831. make . . . householders] decide where poor men shall dwell; i.e. put them in jail.
   833. actions and the cases] legal processes and causes or suits brought into court for decision.
   834. tenants in common] such as hold not by distinct titles, but by unity of possession.
   836. knight's ward] no particular prison seems intended here; rather Nobody is speaking of a division or part of a larger prison.

1.

　I am, sir, a keeper of the Counter, and there
are in our wards above a hundred poor prisoners
that are like ne'er to come forth without
satisfaction.　　　　　　　　　　　　　　　　840

NOBODY.

　But Nobody will be their benefactor. What is yours?

2.

　As many as in the other prison.

NOBODY.

　There's to release them. [He gives them money.]   What
　　　　　　　　　　　　　　　　　　　　　　　　in yours?

3.

　Double the number, and in the gaol.

NOBODY.

　Talk not of the gaol, 'tis full of limetwigs,　　845
lifts, and pickpockets.

1.

　Is it your pleasure, sir, to free them all?

842-43.　Omitted in Simpson.

　　837.　Counter] the name of certain prisons for debtors in
London, Southwark, and some other cities and boroughs.
　　844.　gaol] apparently another division or part of a
larger prison.
　　845.　limetwigs] those whose fingers are limed; thieves.
　　846.　lifts] those who lift; thieves.

NOBODY.

    All that lie in for debt.

2.

    Ten thousand pound, and ten to that will not do it.

NOBODY.

    Nobody, sir, will give a hundred thousand,   850

    ten hundred thousand. Nobody will not have a prisoner,

    because they all shall pray for Nobody.

CLOWN.

    'Tis great pity my master has no body and so

    kind a heart.

        <u>A noise within</u>: <u>Follow, follow, follow.</u>

NOBODY.

    What outcry's that?   855

        <u>Enter</u> Somebody, <u>with two or three.</u>

SOMEBODY.

    That is the gallant, apprehend him straight.

    'Tis he that sows sedition in the land

    Under the color of being charitable.

851-52. <u>printed as verse in</u> Q1 <u>and</u> Simpson. 856. That] Q1; this <u>Simpson.</u>

When search is made for such in every inn,
Though I have seen them housed, the chamberlain   860
For gold will answer there is Nobody.
He for all bankrupts is a common bail,
And when the execution should be served
Upon the sureties, they find Nobody.
In private houses who is so apt to lie   865
As those that have been taught by Nobody?
Servants, forgetful of their master's friends,
Being asked how many were to speak with him
Whilst he was absent, they say Nobody.
Nobody breaks more glasses in a house   870
Than all his wealth hath power to satisfy.
If you will free this city then from shame,
Seize Nobody, and let him bear the blame.

CONSTABLE.
Lay hold upon him.

NOBODY.
What, on Nobody! Give me my sword, my Morglay!   875

---

    860. chamberlain] an attendant at an inn, in charge of the bedchambers.
    864. sureties] the formal engagements entered into for bail.
    865. private houses] as opposed to public houses or inns.
    875. Morglay] the name of the sword belonging to Sir Bevis of Hampton, a knight celebrated in Arthurian Romance and in Polyolbion. Also used allusively for any sword.

My friends, you that do know how innocent I am,

Draw in my quarrel succor Nobody! [Exit jailers.]

What Nobody, but Nobody remaining?

CLOWN.

Yes master, I, Nobody's man.

NOBODY.

Stand to me nobly then, and fear them not;   880

Thy master, Nobody, can take no wounds.

Nobody is no coward, Nobody

Dares fight with all the world.

SOMEBODY.

Upon them then!

A fight betwixt Somebody and Nobody,

Nobody escapes.

What, has he scapt us?

CONSTABLE.

He is gone, my lord.

SOMEBODY.

It shall be thus, now you have seen his shape: 885

Let him be straight imprinted to the life.

*883. with all] withall Q1.

---

880. stand to me] fight stoutly for me.
886. imprinted to the life] portrayed, by some printing process, with life-like presentation.

His picture shall be set on every stall,

And proclamation made that he that takes him,

Shall have a hundred pounds of Somebody.

Country and city I shall thus set free,   890

And have more room to work my villainy.   Exeunt.

[Reenter Nobody.]

NOBODY.

What, are they gone? Then city now adieu,

Since I have taken such great injury

For my good life within thy government.

No more will Nobody be charitable,   895

No more will Nobody relieve the poor.

Honor your lord and master Somebody,

For Somebody is he that wrongs you all.

I'll to the court; the changing of the air

May peradventure change my injuries,   900

And if I speed no better being there,

Yet say that Nobody lived everywhere.   Exit.

*891. And have more] And more in the first Folger copy of Q1 only.

---

    887. stall] a booth or covered stand for the sale of wares at a market or in the open street.
    901. speed] succeed.

[v]   Enter Archigallo.

ARCHIGALLO.

   I was a king, but now I am a slave.
   How happy were I in this base estate
   If I had never tasted royalty.   905
   But the remembrance that I was a king
   Unseasons the content of poverty. [Horns sounded
                                              within.]
   I hear the hunters' music; here I'll lie
   To keep me out of sight till they pass by. [Withdraws.]

                    Enter Morgan and Malgo.

MORGAN.
   The stag is herded. Come, my lord,   910
   Shall we to horse and single him again?
MALGO.
   Content, the king will chase. The day is spent
   And we have killed no game. To horse, away!
                          [Exeunt.]

*903. am a slave] Simpson; am slave Q1.
___

   910. herded] placed in a herd.
   911. single] to separate one from the herd.

Enter Elidure.

ELIDURE.

Herded? Go single him, or couple straight,

He will not fall today. What fellow's this   915

ARCHIGALLO [*coming forward*].

I am a man.

ELIDURE.

A banished man I think;

My brother Archigallo, is't not so?

ARCHIGALLO.

'Tis so, I am thy brother, Elidure.

All that thou hast is mine; the crown is mine,

Thy royalty is mine, these hunting pleasures   920

Thou dost usurp; ambitious Elidure,

I was a king!

ELIDURE.

And I may be a wretch. Poor Archigallo,

The sight of thee that wert my sovereign,

In this estate, draws rivers from mine eyes.   925

Will you be king again? If they agree,

I'll redeliver all my royalty,

Save what a second brother and a subject

---

914. *couple straight*] to match or engage in a battle immediately.

Keeps in an humble bosom, for I swear

The crown is yours that Elidure doth wear. 930

ARCHIGALLO.

Then give it me; use not the common sleights,

To pity one and keep away his right.

Seest thou these rags? Do they become my person?

O Elidure, take pity on my state,

Let me not still live thus infortunate. 935

ELIDURE.

Alas, if pity could procure your good,

Instead of water, I'd weep tears of blood

To express both love and pity. Say, dear brother,

I should uncrown myself; the angry peers

Will never let me reach the imperial wreath 940

To Archigallo's head. There's ancient Cornwell,

Stout Martianus, Morgan, and bold Malgo,

From whom you took the pleasant Southern Isle,

Will never kneel to you. What should I say,

Your tyranny was cause of your decay. 945

ARCHIGALLO.

What, shall I die then? Welcome be that fate,

Rather than still live in this wretched state.

---

931. <u>sleights</u>] tricks, stratagems.
938. <u>say</u>] suppose.

Enter Cornwell, Martianus, Morgan, *and* Malgo.

CORNWELL.

    Yonder's the king. My sovereign, you have lost

    The fall of a brave stag; he's dead, my liege.

    What fellow's this?

ELIDURE.

                  Knowest him not, Cornwell?   950

CORNWELL.

    No, my liege, not I.

ARCHIGALLO.

                  I am thy king.

ELIDURE.

    'Tis Archigallo, man!

CORNWELL.

    Thou art no king of mine, thou art a traitor.

    Thy life is forfeit by thy stay in Britain.

    Wert thou not banished?

ELIDURE.

                  Noble Cornwell, speak   955

    More gently, or my piteous heart will break.

    Lord Martianus, Morgan, and the rest,

    I am aweary of my government,

    And willingly resign it to my brother.

MARTIANUS.

    Your brother was a tyrant, and my knee   960

  Shall never bow to wrong and tyranny.

ELIDURE.

  Yet look upon his misery, his tears

  Argue repentance. Think not, honored lords,

  The fear of dangers waiting on my crown

  Makes me so willing to resign the same,   965

  For I am loved, I know; but justice bids

  I make a resignation. 'Tis his right,

  My call's but usurpation.

CORNWELL.

      Elidure

  If you are weary of your government,

  We'll set the crown upon a stranger's head   970

  Rather than Archigallo. Hark ye lords,

  Shall we make him our king we did depose?

  So might our heads be chopped off. I'll lose mine

  Ere my poor country shall endure such wrongs

  As that injurious tyrant plagues her with.   975

MORGAN.

  Keep still your crown, my liege; happy is Britain

  Under the government of Elidure.

ARCHIGALLO.

  Let it be so,

  Death is the happy period of all woe.

---

  979. <u>period</u>] end.

The wretch that's torn upon the torturing rack   980
Feels not more devilish torment than my heart,
When I but call to mind my tyranny.
I record heaven, my lords, my brother's sight,
The pity that he takes of my distress,
Your love and true allegiance unto him,   985
Hath wrought in me a reconciled spirit.
I do confess my sin, and freely say,
I did deserve to be deposed.

ELIDURE.

Alas good Prince; my honorable lords,
Be not flint-hearted, pity Archigallo.   990
I know his penitential words proceed
From a remorseful spirit; I'll engage
My life upon his righteous government.
Good Cornwell, gentle Martianus, speak;
Shall Archigallo be your king again?   995

ARCHIGALLO.

By heaven, I not desire it.

ELIDURE.

     See, my lords,
He's not ambitious. As thou lov'st me, Cornwell,
As thou didst love our father, let his son

---

 983. I record heaven] "I call heaven to witness . . ."--Gibbs in Simpson.

    Be righted; give him back the government
    You took from him.   1000
CORNWELL.
    What should I say? Faith, I shall fall aweeping;
    Therefore speak you.
ELIDURE.
              Lord Martianus, speak.
MARTIANUS.
    What say these lords that have been wronged by him?
ELIDURE.
    Morgan and Malgo, all I have in Britain
    Shall be engaged to you, that Archigallo   1005
    Will never more oppress you, nor impose
    Wrong on the meanest subject in the land.
MORGAN.
    Then we'll embrace his government.
ELIDURE.
                    Says Malgo so?
MALGO.
    I do, my lord.
ELIDURE.
              What says Martianus?
MARTIANUS.
    Faith, as my Lord of Cornwell.   1010
CORNWELL.
    I say that I am sorry he was bad,

And now am glad he's changed; his wickedness

We punished, and his goodness there's great reason

Should be rewarded. Therefore, lords, set on

To York then, to his coronation. 1015

ELIDURE.

Then happy Elidurus, happy day

That takes from me a kingdom's cares away.

ARCHIGALLO.

And happy Archigallo, that have ranged

From sin to sin, and now at last am changed.

My lords and friends, the wrongs that you have seen 1020

In me my future virtues shall redeem.

Come, gentle brother; pity, that should rest

In women most, is harbored in thy breast.

         Exeunt [omnes].

[vi] Enter Queen, Lady Elidure, and Flatterer.

LADY.

Come, have you done your task? Now do you see

What 'tis to be so proud of majesty? 1025

We must take up your glove, and not be thought

Worthy the name of sister. Thus, you minx,

I'll teach you ply your work, and thank me too.

1027. minx] a saucy, bold girl.

QUEEN.

    This pains will be your own another day.

    Insulting, over-proud, ambitious woman--   1030

    Queen I disdain to call thee-thou dost wrong

    Thy brother's wife, indeed thy king's espoused,

    And mauger all thy tyranny, I swear

    Rather than still live thus, I'll perish here.

SICOPHANT.

    You are not wise, dejected as you are,   1035

    To bandy braves against her majesty.

    You must consider you are now her subject;

    Your tongue is bounded by the awe of duty.

    Fie, fie, I needs must chide you, since I see

    You are so saucy with her sovereignty.   1040

QUEEN.

    Time was, base spaniel, thou didst fawn as much

    On me as now thou strivest to flatter her.

    O God, that one born noble should be so base,

    His generous blood to scandal all his race.

*1029. Q1 assigns to Lady.

    1029. This] read These.
    1033. mauger] in spite of.
    1036. braves] challenges.
    1041. spaniel] a fawning person.
    1043. be so base] Simpson says "be" is superfluous, and reads base as "abase." I read base as contemptible, low. cf. l. 1041.
    1044. generous] of noble lineage.
    1044. race] a set or class of persons.

LADY.
>My lord, if she continue these proud terms, 1045
>I give you liberty to punish her.
>I'll not maintain my prisoner and my slave
>To rail against anyone that honors me.

>*Enter Morgan and Malgo.*

MORGAN.
>Health to the queen, and happiness to her
>That must change states with you, and once more reign 1050
>Queen of this land.

QUEEN.
>Speak that again. Oh I will bless my fate,
>If once more I supply my former state.

MALGO.
>Long may your highness live! Your banished lord
>Is by his brother, Elidurus, seated 1055
>Once more in Britain's throne.

LADY.
>O I could tear my hair! Base Elidure,
>To wrong himself and make a slave of me.

*1052. Oh] o Q1.

1053. supply] to fill a place or position.

QUEEN.

    Now, minion, I'll cry quittance with your pride,

    And make you stoop at our imperial side.   1060

    But tell me, Morgan, by what accident

    You met with my beloved Archigallo.

MORGAN.

    Even in the woods where we did hunt the stag,

    There did the tender-hearted Elidure

    Meet his distressed brother, and so wrought   1065

    By his importunate speech with all his peers,

    That after much denial, yet at last

    They yielded their allegiance to your lord,

    Whom now we must acknowledge our dread king

    And you our princely queen.   1070

LADY.

    Thou screech owl, raven, ugly-throated slave,

    There's for thy news.   [strikes him.]

QUEEN.

        Restrain her, good my lord.

1072. strikes him] Simpson.

    1059. cry quittance] to make oneself even with, to make full retaliation.
    1065-66. wrought . . . peers] and he so moved all his peers with his persistent speech.
    1071. screech owl] applied to a bearer of evil tidings, from the discordant cry of the barn owl, supposed to be an evil omen.
    1071. raven] a curvine bird with a raucous voice.

SICOPHANT.

    Fie madam, fie, fore God you are to blame,

    In presence of my sovereign lady queen

    To be thus rude; it would become you better   1075

    To show more duty to her majesty.

LADY.

    O monstrous! Was not I thy queen but now?

SICOPHANT.

    Yes, when your husband was my king you were.

    But now the stream is turned, and the state's current

    Runs all to Archigallo. Blame not me;

    Wisdom ne'er loved declined majesty.

        Enter Archigallo *crowned*, Elidure, Peridure,

        Vigenius, Cornwell, Martianus, *and others*.

QUEEN.

    Welcome from banishment, my loving lord.

    Your kingly presence raps my soul to heaven.

ARCHIGALLO.

    To heaven and my kind brother Elidure,

    Fair queen, we owe chief thanks for this our

                           greatness.   1085

    Next them, these honorable lords.

    1083.   *raps*] affects with rapture, transports.
    1086.   *Next them*] next to them.

CORNWELL.

                              Great queen,
Once more the tribute of our bended knees
We pay to you, and humbly kiss your hand.

MARTIANUS.

   So doth Martianus.

PERIDURE.

                  And I.

VIGENIUS.

                           And I.

QUEEN.

   Our brothers, by how much that name exceeds   1090
   The name of lord, so much the more this duty
   Deserves requital; thanks both, and thanks to all.

ARCHIGALLO.

   Set on there.   <u>Exeunt all but</u> Lady Elidure
                                  <u>and</u> Sicophant.

SICOPHANT.

   Madam, you are not wise to grieve at that
   Heaven hath decreed, and the state yielded to.   1095
   No doubt her majesty will use you well.

LADY.

   Well sayest thou? No, I look that she should treble
   All the disgraces I have laid on her.
   I shall turn laundress now, and learn to starch,

And set, and poke, and pocket up such baseness   1100
As never princess did.   Did you observe
What looks I cast at Elidure, my husband?
SICOPHANT.
Your looks declared the passion of your heart,
They were all fire.
LADY.
                Would they had burnt his eyes out,
That hath eclipsed our state and majesty.   1105
        <u>Enter</u> Queen, Morgan, <u>and</u> Malgo.
Queen.
Bring hither the proud wife of Elidure.
SICOPHANT.
It shall be done.
QUEEN.
Our shoestring is untied; stoop, minion, stoop.
LADY.
I'll rather stoop to death, thou moon-like queen,
New changed, and yet so proud.   There's those are made

  1100. <u>set</u>] to pleat a ruff or gown, or to make a color fast or permanent.
  1100. <u>poke</u>] to form the folds in a ruff with a poking stick.
  1100. <u>pocket up</u>] submit to, endure meekly.

For flexure, let them stoop; thus much I'll do.

[a stiff curtsy.]

You are my queen, 'tis but a debt I owe.

QUEEN.

Bring me the work there. I will task you to

That by the hour; spin it, I charge you, do.

LADY.

A distaff and a spindle, so indeed.   1115

I told you this, Diana be my speed.

MORGAN.

Yet for his princely worth that made you queen,

Respect her as the wife of Elidure.

Enter Cornwell.

CORNWELL.

Where's the queen?

1111. flexure] the action of bending.
1111. S.D.] "Probable stage action of stiffish obeisence here (as contrasted with stooping to tie the Queen's shoe. . . ." Gibbs in Simpson.
1115. distaff] a cleft stick about three feet long, on which, in spinning, wool or flax was wound.
1115. spindle] An instrument used in spinning consisting of a slender rounded rod, tapering towards each end, which is made to revolve and twist into thread the fibres drawn out of a bunch of wool, flax, or other material.
1116. Diana be my speed] There seems to be no reason to invoke Diana here. The playwright was probably thinking of the goddess of such domestic skills as spinning, who is Minerva, not Diana.

QUEEN.

   What news with Cornwell? Why so sad, my lord?   1120

CORNWELL.

   Your husband on the sudden is fallen sick.

QUEEN.

   How, sick?

LADY.

   Now if it be thy will, sweet blessed heaven,

   Take him to mercy.

QUEEN.

   Do not hear her prayers, heaven, I beseech thee.   1125

Enter Martianus.

MARTIANUS.

   Madam, his highness—

QUEEN.

                Is he alive or dead?

MARTIANUS.

   Dead, madam.

QUEEN.

   O my heart!   [*she faints.*]

CORNWELL.

   Look to the queen, let us not lose her too.

   She breathes, stand off! Where be those women

                            there?   1130

Good queen that shall be, lend's a helping hand,
Help to unlace her.

LADY.
     I'll see her burst first.

QUEEN.
Now as you love me, let no helping hand
Preserve life in me; I had rather die
Than lose the title of my sovereignty.   1135

LADY.
Take back your distaff, yet we'll stay our rage.
We will forbear our spleen for charity
And love unto the dead, till you have hearsed
Your husband's bones. Conduct her, lords, away;
Our pride, though eager, yet for food shall stay. 1140

SICOPHANT.
Wilt please your high imperial majesty
Command my service? I am humble yours.

LADY.
We do command what we well know you'll do,
Follow the strongest part, and cleave thereto.

      <u>Exeunt.</u>

1137. <u>spleen</u>] violent ill-nature.
1138. <u>hearsed</u>] buried.
1140. <u>eager</u>] hungry, full of keen desire.

[vii]   Enter Elidure crowned, all the
              lords and ladies, attendants.

ELIDURE.

    Once more our royal temples are engirt   1145

    With Britain's golden wreath. All-seeing heaven,

    Witness I not desire this sovereignty,

    But since this kingdom's good, and your decrees,

    Have laid this heavy load of common care

    On Elidure, we will discharge the same   1150

    To your content, I hope, and this land's fame.

    Our brother once interred, we will not stay,

    But then to Troynovant we'll speed, away.

                  Exeunt [omnes].

[viii]   Enter two porters.

1 PORTER.

    Come fellow porter, now the court is here,

    Our gains will fly upon us like a tide.   1155

    Let us make use of time, and whilst there's plenty

    Stirring in court, still labor to increase

*1149. heavy] Simpson; heaven Q1.

    1153. Troynovant] the name given to London in the early Chronicles.
    1153.1. porters] gate-keepers.
    1155. fly upon] rush upon.

The wealth which by our office we have got.

2 PORTER.

Out of our large allowance we must save.

Of thousands that pass by us, and our office, 1160

We will give entertainment to Nobody.

<u>Enter</u> Nobody.

NOBODY.

My name is Nobody.

1 PORTER.

You are welcome, sir. Ere you peruse the court,

Taste the king's beer here at the porter's lodge.

A dish of beer for Master Nobody. 1165

NOBODY.

I thank you sir.

2 PORTER.

Here, Master Nobody, with all my heart,

A full carouse, and welcome to our office.

NOBODY.

I thank you sir, and were your beer Thames water,

1161. <u>entertainment</u>] provisions for the wants of a guest.
1163. <u>peruse</u>] to survey, consider in detail.
1165. <u>dish</u>] a hollow vessel used for drinking.
1168. <u>full carouse</u>] a full draught of liquor drunk to one's health.

    Yet Nobody would pledge you. To you, sir.   1170

1 PORTER.

    You are a stranger here, how in the city?

    Have you been long in town?

NOBODY.

    Ay sir, too long, unless my entertain

    Had been more pleasing, for my life is sought.

    I am a harmless, well-disposed, plain man,   1175

    That injure none, yet whatsoe'er is done

    Amiss in London is imposed on me.

    Be it lying, secret theft, or anything

    They call abuse, 'tis done by Nobody.

    I am pursued by all, and now am come   1180

    To see what safety is within the court

    For a plain fellow.

2 PORTER.

                        You are welcome hether, sir.

    Methinks you do look wild, as if you wanted

    sufficient sleep.

NOBODY.

                    O do not blame me, sir,

1171. how] Q1; Simpson suggests reading now.

    1170. pledge you] drink to your health.
    1175. well-disposed] having a favorable disposition.
    1175. plain] honest, straightforward.
    1183. wild] extremely irritated or vexed.

Being pursued I fled. Coming through Paul's, 1185
There Nobody kneeled down to say his prayers,
And was devout, I wis. Coming through Fleet Street,
There at a tavern door two swaggerers
Were fighting. Being attached, 'twas asked who gave
The first occasion; 'twas answered Nobody, 1190
The guilt was laid on me, which made me fly
To the Thames' side, desired a waterman
To row me thence away to Charing Cross.
He asked me for his fare, I answered him
I had no money. What's your name? quoth he; 1195
I told him Nobody; then he bade me welcome,
Said he would carry Nobody for nothing.
From thence I went
To see the law courts held at Westminster.
There meeting with a friend, I straight was asked 1200
If I had any suit. I answered, yes,
Marry, I wanted money. Sir, quoth he,
For you, because your name is Nobody,
I will solicit law, and Nobody,

1187. Fleet Street] "In the early chronicles of London many allusions were made to the deeds of violence done in this street"--The New Century Cyclopedia of Names.
    1189. attached] arrested.
    1190. occasion] offence.
    1192. side] bank.
    1192. waterman] a boatman, especially in London.

Assure yourself, shall thrive by suits in law.
I thanked him, and so came to see the court,
Where I am very much beholding to your kindness.

1 PORTER.
And, Master Nobody, you are very welcome.
Good fellow, lead him to the Hall.
Will you walk near the court?

NOBODY.
       I thank you sir. 1210

Exeunt Nobody *and* porters.

[ix]   Enter Somebody *and a* braggart.

SOMEBODY.
Fie, what a toil it is to find out Nobody.
I have dogged him very close, yet he is got into
the court before me.
Sir, you have sworn to fight with Nobody;
Do you stay here and watch at the court gate, 1215
And when you meet him challenge him the field,
Whilst I set lime twigs for him in all offices.
If either you or I but prosper right,

1212. he is] Q1; is he Simpson.

 1216. challenge him the field] to summon to fight.
 1217. lime twigs] a twig smeared with birdlime for catching birds, here used figuratively.

He needs must fall by policy or sleight.

                     <u>Exit</u> [Somebody].

BRAGGART.

I would this roundman Nobody would come.   1220

I, that profess much valor yet have none,

Cannot but be too hard for Nobody,

For what can be in Nobody, unless

He be so called because he is all spirit?

Or say he be all spirit; wanting limbs,   1225

How can this spirit hurt me? Sure he dies,

And by his death my fame shall mount the skies.

      <u>Enter</u> Nobody [<u>stopped</u> <u>by</u> Braggart].

NOBODY.

By thy leave, my sweet friend,

There's for thy farewell.   [<u>gives</u> <u>him</u> <u>money</u>.]

BRAGGART.

Stay.   1230

NOBODY.

That's but one word; let two go to the bargain, if

it please you. Why should I stay?

BRAGGART.

I challenge thee.

1219. policy] political cunning.
1231. <u>to</u> <u>the</u> <u>bargain</u>] in addition, besides.

NOBODY.

I may choose whither I'll answer your challenge, by
your leave.   1235

BRAGGART.

I'll have thee pictured as thy picute, unless thou
answer me.

NOBODY.

For what, sir? Pray, why would you have me printed?

BRAGGART.

For cowardice.

NOBODY.

Methinks your picutre would do better for the   1240
picutre of cowardice than mine, sir, but pray,
what's your will with me?

BRAGGART.

Thou has abused one Somebody.

NOBODY.

So have my betters abused Somebody in their time.

BRAGGART.

I'll fight with thee for that   1245

NOBODY.

Alas, sir, I am Nobody at fighting, yet thus much

1234. <u>whither</u>] in what place; also a form of whether,
meaning if.

let me tell you, Nobody cannot run away; I
cannot budge.

BRAGGART.

Prepare thee then, for I will spit thy body upon
this weapon.   1250

NOBODY.

Nay by faith, that you cannot, for I have no body.

BRAGGART.

Thy bowels then.

NOBODY.

They are the fairer mark a great deal; come on sir,
come on.

BRAGGART.

Have at thy belly.   1255

NOBODY.

You must either hit that or nothing.

BRAGGART.

I'll kill and quarter thee.

NOBODY.

You'll hardly find my joints, I think, to quarter me,
I am so well fed. Come on sir.

Fight, Nobody <u>is</u> <u>down</u>.

BRAGGART.

Now thou art at my mercy.   1260

NOBODY.

What, are you the better to have Nobody at your mercy?

BRAGGART.

I'll kill thee now.

NOBODY.

I think you'll sooner kill me than anybody,

But let me rise again.

BRAGGART.

No, I will let Nobody rise.   1265

NOBODY.

Why then let me, sir, I am Nobody.

Enter Clown [behind].

CLOWN.

How now? O fates O heavens is not that my

master? What shall I do? Be valiant and rescue

my sweet master.   [Coming forward.]

Avaunt thou pagen, pug, whate'er thou be!   1270

Behold I come to set thy prisoner free.

BRAGGART.

Fortune, that giddy goddess, hath turned her wheel.

I shall be matched, thus will I gore you both. Hold

1270. pug] punk, harlot.
1272. giddy] whirling with bewildering rapidity.

captains, not Hercules himself would fight with

two. I yield. 1275

CLOWN.

'Twas your best course; down, vassal, down, and kiss

my pump.

BRAGGART.

'Tis base, O base.

CLOWN.

Zounds, I'll nail thy lips to limbo unless thou kiss.

BRAGGART.

'Tis done. 1280

NOBODY.

Thanks, honest servant.

CLOWN.

Zounds, if I say I'll do't, I'll do't indeed.

NOBODY.

For this I'll carry thee into the court,

Where thou shalt see thy master, Nobody,

Hath friends will bid him welcome. So farewell. 1285

CLOWN.

Farewell, Master Braggart, farewell, farewell.

Exeunt [Nobody *and* Clown].

1274. captains] a familiar term of address.

BRAGGART.

    I'll follow. I shall meet with Somebody

    That will revenge. I'll plot, and er't be long,

    I'll be revenged on Nobody for this wrong.

                                                      Exit.

[x] _Enter_ Vigenius, Peridure, _and the queen._

QUEEN.

    Your hopes are great, fair brothers, and your names   1290

    Shall, if in this you be advised by us,

    Be ranked in scroll of all the British kings.

    Oh take upon you this so weighty charge,

    Too great to be discharged by Elidure.

VIGENIUS.

    Dear sister Queen, how are we bound to you,   1295

    In nearer bonds than a fraternal league,

    For this your royal practice to raise us

    Unto the height of honor and estate.

    Let me no longer breathe a prince on earth,

    Or think me worthy of your regal blood,   1300

    If we embrace not this high motion.

PERIDURE.

    Embrace it brother. We are all on speed;

1290-91. _printed as prose_ in Q1.

My princely though inflamed with ardency
Of this imperial state and sceptered rule,
My kingly brows itch for a stately crown, 1305
This hand to bear a round monarchal globe,
This the bright sword of justice and stern awe.
Dear sister, you have made me all on fire,
My kingly thoughts beyond their bounds aspire.
VIGENIUS.
How shall we quit your love when we ascend 1310
The state of Elidure?
QUEEN.
                    All that I crave
Is but to make the imperious queen my slave,
That she that above justice now commands
May taste new thraldom at our royal hands.
PERIDURE.
The queen is yours. The king shall be deposed, 1315
And she disgraded from all sovereignty.
QUEEN.
That I might live to see that happy hour,
To have that stern commandress in my power.

1303. ardency] intense eagerness.
1310. quit] repay.
1312. imperious] overbearing.
1316. disgraded] formally deposed.

VIGENIUS.

    She's doomed already and at your dispose,

    And we prepared for speedy execution   1320

    Of any plot that may avail our pomp,

    Or throne us in the state of Brittany.

           <u>Enter</u> Morgan <u>and</u> Malgo.

PERIDURE.

    Here comes the lords of this pretended league.

    How goes our hope? Speak, valiant English peers,

    Are we in way of sovereignty, or still stand we   1325

    Subjects unto the awe of Elidure?

MORGAN.

    Long live the valiant brothers of the king,

    With mutual love to wear the British crown.

    Two thousand soldiers have I brought from Wales

    To wait upon the princely Peridure.   1330

MALGO.

    As many of my bold confederates

    Have I drawn from the South to swear allegiance

    To young Vigenius.

VIGENIUS.

           Do but call me king;

    1323.   <u>comes</u>] read come.
    1323.   <u>pretended</u>] intended, proposed.

The charming Spheres so sweetly cannot sing.

MALGO.

To King Vigenius.

VIGENIUS.

      Oh, but where's our crown, 1335

That make knees humble when their sovereigns frown?

MALGO.

King Elidurus shall his state resign.

PERIDURE.

Say Morgan so, and Britain's rule is mine.

MORGAN.

King Peridure shall reign.

PERIDURE.

      And sit in state.

MORGAN.

And thousand subjects on his glory wait. 1340

PERIDURE.

Then they that lifts us to the imperial seat,

Our powers and will shall study to make great.

VIGENIUS.

And thou that raisest us, as our best friend,

Shall, as we mount, the like degrees ascend.

  1334. charming Spheres] the enthralling music of the Spheres
  1336. make] read makes.
  1341. lifts] read lift.

QUEEN.

    When will you give the attempt?

PERIDURE.

                         Now, royal sister,   1345

    Before the king have notice of our plot,

    Before the lords that love his government

    Prepare their opposition.

VIGENIUS.

                      Well determined,

    And like a king in <u>esse</u>, now, this night,

    Let's make a hostile uproar in the court,   1350

    Surprise the king, make seizure of the crown,

    Lay hands upon the Council, lest they scape

    To levy forces. Those lords

    That serve the king, and with austere reproofs

    Punish the hateful vices of the land,   1355

    Must not awe us; they shall not reign. We will

    Those that applaud us raise; despise us, kill.

PERIDURE.

    I see a kind of state appear already

    In thy majestic brow. Call in the soldiers; [enter

                                                   <u>soldiers.</u>]

    Man the court gates, barricade all the streets,   1360

    1349. <u>in</u> esse] in actual existence.

Defend the ways, the lanes and passages,
And girt the palace with a treble wall
Of armed soldiers; and in dead of night,
When all the peers lie drowned in golden sleep,
Sound out a sudden and a shrill alarum   1365
To maze them in the midst of horrid dreams.

VIGENIUS.

The king and crown is ours!

QUEEN.

        The queen I claim.
It shall go hard, but I the shrew will tame.

PERIDURE.

Trumpets and drums, your dreadful clamors sound!

VIGENIUS.

Proclaim me captive, or a king new-crowned!   1370

  *Alarum, they watch the doors. Enter at
  one door Cornwell, [stopped by Peridure].*

CORNWELL.

Treason! Treason!

*1361. lanes] suggested by Simpson; lands Q1.   *1368. Q1 assigns to Peridure.

 1361. ways] passages left between walls or buildings.
 1365. alarum] alarm, a warning sound of danger.

PERIDURE.

                Thou art mine, whate'er thou be.

CORNWELL.

  Prince Peridure!

PERIDURE.

                I, Cornwell, and thy king.

CORNWELL.

  He discords taught that taught thee so to sing.

        Alarum, <u>enter at another door</u> Martianus,

                [<u>stopped by</u> Vigenius].

MARTIANUS.

  Who stops this passage?

VIGENIUS.

                Martianus, we.

MARTIANUS.

  Vigenius!

VIGENIUS.

        Unto whom thou owest thy knee.   1375

MARTIANUS.

  My knee to none but Elidure shall bend.

VIGENIUS.

  Our reign beginning hath when his line's end.

    1377. <u>when . . . end</u>] when his line of succession is ended.

> Alarum, enter at another door [Lady] Elidure,
> stopped by the queen.

LADY.

What trait'rous hand dares interdict our way?

QUEEN.

Why that dare ours, 'tis we command thee stay.

LADY.

Are we not queen?

QUEEN.

     Is't you? Then happily met. 1380
I have owed you long, and now I'll pay that debt.

LADY.

Vild traitress, darest thou lay a violent hand
On us thy queen?

QUEEN.

    We dare command thee stand.
Thou wast a queen, but now thou art a slave.

LADY.

Before such bondage, grant me, heaven, a grave. 1385

> Alarum, enter Elidure.

1382-83. hand/On us] hand on/us Q1.

 1378. interdict] forbid, prohibit.

ELIDURE.

    What seek ye lords? What mean these loud alarums

    In the still silence of this honeyed night?

PERIDURE.

    King, we seek thee.

VIGENIUS.

                    And more, we seek thy crown.

ELIDURE.

    Why princely brothers, is it not our own?

    That 'tis ours we plead the law of kings,   1390

    The gift of heaven, and the antiquity on earth,

    Election from them both.

VIGENIUS.

    We plead our powers and strength, we two must reign.

PERIDURE.

    We were born to rule, and homage we disdain.

CORNWELL.

    Do not resign, good king.

PERIDURE.

                    How, saucy lord?   1395

CORNWELL.

    I'll keep still thy crown.

    1387. honeyed] sweet, mellifluous.

    1391. The gift . . . earth] in apposition to "the law of kings."

    1391. antiquity] precedents, customs of earlier times.

PERIDURE.

    I say that word shall cost old Cornwell's life.

CORNWELL.

    Tush, this for care.

    Tyrants good subjects kills, and traitors spare.

VIGENIUS.

    Wilt thou submit thy crown?

MARTIANUS.

                       Dread sovereign, no!   1400

VIGENIUS.

    He hates his own life that adviseth so.

MARTIANUS.

    I hate all traitors, and had rather die

    Than see such wrong done to his sovereignty.

QUEEN.

    Give up thy state to these two princely youths,

    And thy resignment shall preserve thy life.   1405

LADY.

    Wilt thou so much wrong both thy self and wife?

    Hast lived a king, and canst thou die a slave?

    A royal seat doth ask a royal grave.

    Though thousand swords thy present safety ring,

    Thou that hast been a monarch, die a king!   1410

    1399. <u>Tyrants</u> . . . <u>kills</u>] tyrants kill good subjects.

QUEEN.

    Whether he live or die, thou sure shalt be

    No longer queen, but vassal unto me.

    I'll make ye now my drudge.

LADY.

                    How, minion, thine?

QUEEN.

    Th'art no more queen, thy husband must resign.

CORNWELL.

    Resign? To whom?

PERIDURE.

                    I am one.

VIGENIUS.

                    And I another.   1415

LADY.

    Canst be so base to see a younger brother,

    Nay, two young boys placed in thy throne of state,

    And thou their sudden in their trains to wait?

    I'll die before I endure it.

1411-12. printed as prose in Q1.

    1413. drudge] one employed in mean, servile work.
    1418. sudden] Simpson conjectures soudan, sultan, or sovraine from the original spelling sodaine. However the playwright here is using the adjective as a noun to mean a servant who is quick to perform, prompt.

PERIDURE.
                    So shall all
    That do not prostrate to our homage fall.   1420
    Shall they not, brother king?
VIGENIUS.
                                        They shall, by heaven.
MARTIANUS.
    Come, kill me first.
CORNWELL.
                    Nay, make the number even
    And kill me too, for I am pleased to die
    Rather than this endure.
LADY.
                        The third am I.
QUEEN.
    Nay, strike her first.
PERIDURE.
                        Rage give my fury way.   1425
VIGENIUS.
    Strike, valiant brother king!
ELIDURE.
                            Yet hear me, stay!
PERIDURE.
    Be brief, for God's sake, then.

    1425. <u>way</u>] a means to achieve my end.

ELIDURE.

    O heaven, that men so much should covet care.

    Scepters are golden baits, the outsides fair;

    But he that swallows this sweet sugared pill,   1430

    'Twill make him sick with troubles that grow still.

    Alas, you seek to ease me, being wearied,

    And lay my burthen on your able loins.

    My unambitious thoughts have been long tired

    With this great charge, and now they rest desired,   1435

    And see the kind youths, coveting my peace,

    Bring me of all these turmoils free release.

    Here, take my crown.

LADY.

                Wilt thou be made a stale?

    Shall this proud woman and these boys prevail?

    Shall I for them be made a public scorn?   1440

    Oh hadst thou buried been as soon as born,

    How happy had I been.

ELIDURE.

              Patience, sweet wife;

    Thinkst thou I priase my crown above thy life?

    1431. still] continually.
    1435. now . . . desired] the unambitious thoughts I have longed for are now mine and are fulfilled.
    1436. coveting] desirous of peace for Elidure, not for themselves.
    1438. stale] an accomplice of a thief.
    1443. praise] to value, esteem; to prize.

No, take it lords, it hath my trouble been,

And for this crown, oh give me back my queen.   1445

QUEEN.

Nay, she's bestowed on me.

ELIDURE.

                Then what you please;

Here, take my trouble, and resign your ease.

SICOPHANT.

My lords, receive the crown of Elidure.

Fair hopefull blossoms of our future peace,

Happy am I, that I but live to see   1450

The land ruled by your double sovereignty.

VIGENIUS.

Now let the king descend to be disposed of

At our high pleasure. Come, give me the crown.

PERIDURE.

Why you the crown, good brother, more than we?

VIGENIUS.

We'll prove it, how it fits our kingly temples,   1455

And how our brow becomes a wreath so fair.

PERIDURE.

Shall I see you crowned, and myself stand bare?

Rather this wreath majestic let me try,

1455. prove it] prove.

And sit inthroned in pompous majesty.

VIGENIUS.

And I attend, whilst you ascend the throne   1460

Where, had we right, we should sit crowned alone?

PERIDURE.

Alone! Dar'st thou usurp upon my right?

VIGENIUS [aside].

I durst do much, had I but power and might.

But wanting that,--Comé, let us reign together,

Both kings, and yet the rich crown worn by neither. 1465

PERIDURE.

Content. The king doth on our sentence wait;

To doom him, come, let's take our double state.

What, shall he live, or die?

ELIDURE.

I know not how I should deserve to die.

LADY.

Yes, to let two such usurpers live.   1470

SICOPHANT.

Nay, madam, now I needs must tell your grace,

You wrong these kings, forget both time and place.

It is not as it was; now you must bow

Unto this double state; I'll show you how.

LADY.

    Base flattering groom, slavish parasite.   1475

VIGENIUS.

    Shall I pronounce his sentence?

PERIDURE.

                      Brother, do.

VIGENIUS.

    Thy life we grant thee, and that woman's too,
    But live divided, you within the tower,
    You prisoner to that princess.

LADY.

                    In her power?

    Oh double slavery!

PERIDURE.

                Convey both hence.   1480

ELIDURE.

    My doom's severer than my small offense. [Exit Elidure,
                                          guarded.]

QUEEN.

    Come, minion, will you go?

LADY.

                      To death, to hell,
    Rather than in thy base subjection dwell.

              [Exit Lady Elidure, Queen, Sicophant.]

    1475. groom] a man of inferior position; a serving man.

VIGENIUS.

    Cornwell and Martianus, you both see
    We are possessed of this imperial seat,   1485
    And you that were sworn liegemen to the crown
    Should now submit to us that owe the same.
    We know without your grave directions
    We cannot with experience guide the land;
    Therefore we'll study to deserve your loves.   1490

PERIDURE.

    'Twas not ambition or the love of state
    That drew us to this business, but the fear
    Of Elidurus' weakness, whom in zeal
    To the whole land we have deposed this day.
    Speak, shall we have your loves?

CORNWELL.

                              My lords, and kings, 1495
    'Tis bootless to contend 'gainst heaven and you.
    Since without our consent the king's deposed,
    And we unable to support his fall,
    Rather than the whole land should shrink
    You shall have my assistance in the state.   1500

MARTIANUS.

    Cornwell and I will bear the selfsame state.

1487. <u>owe</u>] own, possess.
1499. <u>shrink</u>] collapse, give way.

PERIDURE.

    We now are kings indeed and Britain sway

    When Cornwell and his brother viva say.

VIGENIUS.

    Receive our grace, keep still your offices,

    Embrace these peers that raised us to the throne.   1505

    Britain rejoice, and crown this happy year;

    Two sons at once shine in thy royal sphere.

CORNWELL.

    And that's prodigious [Aside] I but wait the time

    To see their sudden fall that swiftly climb.

MARTIANUS.

    My lord, much honor might you win your land   1510

    To give release unto your sister queen,

    Being a lady in the land beloved.

VIGENIUS.

    You have advised us well, it shall be so.

CORNWELL.

    Should you set free the princess, might not she

    Make uproars in the land, and raise the commons   1515

    In the releasement of the captive king?

    1502.   sway] rule
    1503.   viva] used to express good will or approval.
    1506.   crown] endow with honor, dignity.
    1608.   prodigious] unnatural, ominous.

PERIDURE.

Well counseled, Cornwell, she shall live in bondage.

MARTIANUS.

Renown yourself by being kind to her.

CORNWELL.

Secure your state by her imprisonment.

VIGENIUS.

We'll have the queen set free.

PERIDURE.

                                         We'll have her guarded,

With stricter keeping and severer charge.

MARTIANUS.

Will you be braved by one that's but your equal,

Having no more than party government?

CORNWELL.

Or you be scorned by one to you inferior

In general estimation of the land?   1525

VIGENIUS.

Set free the princess; say the king commands.

PERIDURE.

Keep her in thraldom still and captive bands.

VIGENIUS.

We'll not be countermanded.

    1523. <u>party</u>] divided, partial.
    1524. <u>Or you</u>] or will you.

PERIDURE.

    Sir, nor we.

VIGENIUS.

 Before I'll be half a king and controlled

 In any regality, I'll hazard all.   1530

 I'll be complete or none.

PERIDURE.

      Before I'll stand

 Thus for a cipher with my half command,

 I'll venture all my fortunes. [Vigenius <u>sits on the</u>

    <u>throne</u>.] How now, pride,

 Perched on my upper hand?

CORNWELL.

    [Aside] By heaven, well spied.

VIGENIUS.

 'Tis ours by right, and right we will enjoy.   1535

PERIDURE.

 Claimst thou preeminence? Come down, proud boy!

VIGENIUS.

 Then let's try masteries and one conquer all.

 We climbed at once, and we at once will fall.

1530. any] Q1; <u>Simpson suggests</u> my. 1539-40. themselves/
Upon their] themselves upon/their Q1.

 1532. <u>cipher</u>] a person who fills a place, but is of no importance or worth.
 1537. <u>try masteries</u>] have a test of our strengths.

They wrestle and are parted.

PERIDURE.

They that love Peridure divide themselves

Upon their part.

CORNWELL.

That am I.

MORGAN.

And I.   1540

VIGENIUS.

They that love us on this side.

MARTIANUS.

I.

MALGO.

And I.

VIGENIUS.

Then to the field, to set our sister free.

PERIDURE.

By all my hopes, with her I'll captive thee.

VIGENIUS.

Trumpets and drums, triumphant music sing!

PERIDURE.

This day a captive, or a complete king!   1545

Exeunt omnes.

1540. Upon their part] on the side they favor.

[xi]   Alarum, enter Somebody and Sicophant.

SOMEBODY.

  Sir, you have sworn to manage these affairs,
  Even with your best of judgement.

           Enter Clown [unseen].

SICOPHANT.

  I have, provided you will let me share
  Of the grand benefit you get by dice,
  Deceitful cards, and other cozening games   1550
  You bring into the court.

CLOWN.

  O rare! Now shall I find out crab, some
  notable knavery.

SOMEBODY.

  You shall have equal share with Somebody,
  Provided you will help to apprehend   1555
  That Nobody, on whom the guilt shall lie
  Of all those cheating tricks I have devised.

1555-56. apprehend/That Nobody, on] apprehend that Nobody,/ On Q1.

  1552. crab] "Perhaps this is a name for Sycophant, who crawls, and crawls backward, too"--Gibbs.

CLOWN.

O the fates, treason against my master's person!

But I believe Somebody will pay for't; I'll

tickle your long waist for this, i'faith.   1560

SICOPHANT.

Give me some bales of dice. What are these?

SOMEBODY.

Those are called high fulhams.

CLOWN.

I'll fulham you for this.

SOMEBODY.

Those low fulhams.

CLOWN.

They may chance bring you as high as the gallows.   1565

SOMEBODY.

Those demi-bars.

CLOWN.

Great reason you should come to the bar

before the gallows.

    1560. long waist] "Somebody was personated on the stage having a very long body and hardly any legs . . ."--Gibbs.
    1561. bales] sets for any special game.
    1562-64. high fulhams, low fulhams] loaded dice; "high-fullums, which seldom run any other chance than four, five, or six; Low-fullums, which run one, two, and three"--R. Head, The English Rogue, 1665, cited in Eric Partridge, A Dictionary of the Underworld, 1949.
    1566. demi-bars] a kind of false dice on which certain numbers are prevented from turning up.

SOMEBODY.

    Those bar-sizeaces.

CLOWN.

    A couple of asses indeed.   1570

SOMEBODY.

    Those bristle-dice.

CLOWN.

    'Tis like they bristle, for I am sure they'll

    breed anger.

SICOPHANT.

    Now sir, as you have compassed all the dice,

    So I for cards. These for the game at maw;   1575

    All saving one, are cut next under that.

    Lay me the ace of hearts, then cut the cards,

    O your fellow must needs have it in his first trick.

CLOWN.

    I'll teach you a trick for this, i'faith.

    1569. bar-sizeaces] a kind of false dice on which the number six is prevented from turning up.
    1571. bristle-dice] dice into which bristles were fixed to influence their position when thrown.
    1574. compassed] fixed, altered.
    1575. maw] an old card game, played with a piquet pack of thirty-six cards, and by from two to six players.

SICOPHANT.

    These for primero, cut upon the sides,   1580

    As the other on the ends.

CLOWN.

    Mark the end of all this.

SICOPHANT.

    These are for post and pair, these for cent,

    These for new cut.

CLOWN.

    They'll make you cut a feather one day.   1585

SICOPHANT.

    Well, these dispersed, and Nobody,

    Attached for all these crimes, shall be hanged.

CLOWN.

    Ay, or else you shall hang for him.

SICOPHANT.

    Come, shall's about our business?

SOMEBODY.

    Content, let's straight about it.   1590

                Exeunt [Somebody and Sicophant].

    1580. primero] a gambling card game in which four cards were dealt to each player, each card having thrice its ordinary value.
    1580. cut] literally cut, or marked.
    1583-84. post and pair, cent, new cut] all card games.
    1585. cut a feather] Tilley, F160; cf. Tilley, H32.
    1589. shall's] shall us, shall we be.

CLOWN [coming forward].

O, my heart, that it was my fortune to hear all this!
But beware a lucky man whilst you live. Alas,
if I had not rescued my master, the swaggering
fellow would have made Nobody of him. Again,
if I had not overheard this treason to his   1595
person, these cony-catching knaves would have
made less than Nobody of him; for indeed they
would have hanged him. But here's my master.
O sweet master, how cheer you?

Enter Nobody.

NOBODY.

O excellent, admirable, and beyond comparison.   1600
I think my shape enchants them.

CLOWN.

I think not so, for if I were a lady I
should never abide you. But master, I
can tell you rare news; you must be
apprehended for a cheater, a cozener, a libeler, 1605
and I know not what.

NOBODY.

Not I, I am an innocent; no cheater, no cozener,

    1596. cony-catching] swindling, gulling.
    1603. abide] endure, bear, with a pun on the past tense form, "abed".

but a simple honest man, hunted from place to place by Somebody.

CLOWN.

'Tis true sir, it is one Somebody that would attach   1610
you; therefore look to yourself. But, master, if you
be took, never fear; I heard all their knavery, and
I can clear you, I warrant.

                Enter Somebody and officers.

SOMEBODY.

O have I found you? This is he, my friends,
We have long sought. You know when 'twas inquired   1615
Who brought the false dice and the cheating cards
Into the court, 'twas answered Nobody.

CLOWN [and] NOBODY (q.d. tha.).

I am afraid you'll prove the knave, Somebody.

SOMEBODY.

Lay hold upon him, bear him to the prison.

NOBODY.

To prison, say you well? If I be guilty,   1620

    1613. warrant] guarantee.
    1618. q.d. tha.] q.d. or quasi dictum, as if said; tha. is obscure. The sense of the abbreviation is as if said together or simultaneously; hence perhaps tha. is the abbreviation of the ablative form of tractus, trahum, meaning proceeding continuously.

This fellow is my partner; take him too.

SOMEBODY.

Are you confederate in this treason, sirrah?

CLOWN.

If I be not, sir, Somebody is; but if I be guilty I
must bear, if off with head and shoulders.

SOMEBODY.

To prison with them. Now the bird is caught,   1625
For whom so long through Britain have I sought.

CLOWN.

I believe I have a bird in a box shall catch you
for all this.

SOMEBODY.

Away with them I say!

         Exeunt [omnes].

[xii] Enter severally Peridure, Vigenius, Cornwell,
  Martianus, Morgan, Malgo, with drum and colors.

VIGENIUS.

In arms well met, ambitious Peridure.   1630

PERIDURE.

Vigenius, thou salutes me with a title

1624. if] Q1; it Simpson.   *1627. catch] catcht Q1.

 1624. bear] endure the punishment.
 1625. bird in a box] prey or object of attack cornered
or in a fix, with a probable pun on dice box.

Most proper to thyself.

VIGENIUS.
Art thou not proud?

PERIDURE.

Only to meet thee on this bed of death,
Wherein thy title to the English crown
Shall perish with thyself.

VIGENIUS.
Fair is the end   1635
Of such as die in honorable war,
Oh far more fair than on a bed of down.

MARTIANUS.

War is the soldier's harvest; it cuts down--

PERIDURE.

The lives of such as hinder our renown.

VIGENIUS.

Such as are apt for tumult.

PERIDURE.
Such as you,   1640
That to our lawful sovereign are untrue.

VIGENIUS.

Blushes not Peridure to brave us so?

*1634. thy] the Q1.

PERIDURE.

    Blushes, Vigenius, at thy overthrow.

    Who was't that told me he would submit?

SICOPHANT.

    'Twas I, my lord.

VIGENIUS.

                  Peace, fool; thou dost forget   1645

    'Tis not an hour since, to our princely ear,

    Thous saidst thou did desire us to forbear.

SICOPHANT.

    True, my good lord.

PERIDURE.

                  True that I sought to stay?

VIGENIUS.

    That I would basely my rich'st hopes betray?

SICOPHANT.

    I did it of mine own head to make you friends.   1650

PERIDURE.

    Still playing of the Sicophant.

VIGENIUS.

                            What, still?

1647. did] Q1; didst <u>Simpson</u>. 1648. stay? <u>Simpson</u>;   . Q1.

    1647. <u>Thou saidst thou</u>] Sicophant said Peridure.
    1649. <u>rich'st</u>] richest.
    1650. <u>of mine own head</u>] out of my own thought.

PERIDURE.

    A gloze, I see, to insinuate our good will.

VIGENIUS.

    That whosoever conquered, he might gain--

PERIDURE.

    The favor of us both, that was his train.

VIGENIUS.

    But henceforth we cashier thee from the field.   1655

PERIDURE.

    Never hereafter bear a soldier's shield,

    A soldier's sword, nor any other grace,

    But what is like thine own, a double face.

SICOPHANT.

    Now I beseech Jove hear my prayer, let

    them be both slain in the battle.   1660

                    <u>Exeunt</u> [Sicophant].

PERIDURE.

    If there be any other of his heart,

    We give them free license to depart.

CORNWELL.

    Cornwell hates flattery.

    1652. <u>gloze</u>] a pretense, false show.
    1652. <u>insinuate</u>] to win or gain.
    1654. <u>train</u>] stratagem, scheme.
    1655. <u>cashier</u>] to dismiss from service or command.

MARTIANUS.

                       So does Martianus.

MALGO.

   Malgo is resolute for all affiars.

MORGAN.

   And so is Morgan, for he scorns delays.   1665

VIGENIUS.

   Then where the field consists of such a spirit,

   He that subdues conquers the crown by merit.

PERIDURE.

   That's I.

VIGENIUS.

        'Tis I.

PERIDURE.

               Rivers in blood declare it.

VIGENIUS.

   Grass turn to crimson if Vigenius spare it.

PERIDURE.

   Air be made purple with our reeking gore.   1670

VIGENIUS.

   Follow, my friends.

*1670. PERIDURE Elid. Q1.

   1670. <u>reeking</u>] that which emits vapor or steam.

PERIDURE.

    Conquer, or ne'er give o'er.

        [Exit omnes.]

  Alarum, excursions; Peridure and Vigenius

      fight, and both slain.

  Enter Cornwell, Martianus, Morgan, and Malgo,

      [and soldiers].

MARTIANUS.

  This way I saw Vigenius on the spur.

CORNWELL.

  I Peridurus this way.

MORGAN.

  A strange sight! My lord is breathless!

MALGO.

  My dear lord is dead!   1675

MARTIANUS.

  True brothers in ambition and in death.

CORNWELL.

  Yet we are enemies; why fight we not

  With one another for our generals' loss?

MARTIANUS.

  Too much blood already hath been spent.

  1672. on the spur] at full speed.

                Now, therefore, since the difference in
                                         themselves   1680
    Is reconciled in either's overthrow,
    Let us be as we were before this jar,
    And joining hands like honorable friends,
    Inter their bodies as becomes their state;
    And, which is rare, once more to Elidure,   1685
    Who now in prison leads a wearied life,
    With true submission offer England's crown.
    Of all the changes of tumultuous fate,
    This is most strange, three times to flow in state.
                     Exeunt [omnes, with the bodies].
[xiii]   Enter Queen and Sicophant.
SICOPHANT.
    Madam.   1690
QUEEN.
    You are welcome. What new flatteries
    Are acoining in the mint of that smooth face?
SICOPHANT.
    Where is the Lady Elidure, I pray?

*1688. changes] suggested by Gibbs in Simpson; charges Q1.

    1682. jar] discord.
    1689. flow] like the tide, to ebb and flow in and out of office.
    1692. smooth] seemingly friendly or sincere.

QUEEN.

Amongst my other waiting maids at work.

SICOPHANT.

'Tis well, yet madam, with your gracious leave,   1695
I wish it better.

QUEEN.

What, in love with her?
Canst thou affect such a dejected wretch?
Then I perceive thy flattery is folly,
Or thou't prove honest, loving one so poor.

SICOPHANT.

I know not, madam, what your highness gathers   1700
Out of my troubled words. I love you well,
And though the time should alter, as I am sure
It is impossible, yet I would follow
All your misfortunes with a patient heart.

QUEEN.

I have seen too much of thee to credit thee.   1705

SICOPHANT.

Now, in your height of glory, use your servant
Now, madam, whilst the noble Peridure
That loves you dearer than the British crown,

1697. dejected] lowered in estate.
1699. thou't] thou wilt.

Whilst he's conqueror, use me to destroy

Your greatest enemy, and I will do it. 1710

QUEEN.

Thou wilt not.

SICOPHANT.

Be it Elidure the King,

The prisoner I should say, I'd murder him

To show how much I love your majesty.

QUEEN.

Thou wouldst not poison for me his base queen,

Whom I so often have triumphed o'er. 1715

That torment now is her beatitude,

And tedious unto me.

SICOPHANT.

No more, she's dead.

Enter Lady Elidure.

QUEEN.

See where she comes. Dispatch her presently,

For though the princely Peridure be king,

His brother's death in time will make him odious 1720

Unto his subjects, and they may restore

Mild Elidure again, and then I die.

1717. tedious] annoying, disagreeable.

SICOPHANT.

    Withdraw; she's dead, as surely as you live.

                   [They withdraw.]

LADY.

    What, shall I never from this servitude

    Receive releasant? Evermore be plagued   1725

    With this insulting queen? Is there no change,

    No other alteration in the state?

    I know there is not; I am born to be

    A slave to one baser than slavery.

SICOPHANT.

    I will release you, by a speedy death.   1730

LADY.

    By death! Alas, what tongue pronounced that word?

              [Sicophant comes forward.]

    What, my lord weathercock? Nay, then, I see

    Death in thy mouth is but base flattery.

SICOPHANT.

    By heaven I am sent to kill you.

LADY.

    By whose means?   1735

    1725. releasant] release.
    1732. weathercock] one who is changeable or inconstant.

SICOPHANT.

    By one that will avouch it when 'tis done.

LADY.

    Not the proud queen!

SICOPHANT [drawing Lady Elidure aside].

                    Yes, but I am determined,

    In full amends for all my flattery,

    To save your life, and kill her instantly.

LADY.

    Oh if a devil would undertake that deed,   1740

    I care not though she heard me, I would say

    He were a star more glorious than the day.

SICOPHANT.

    And would you for that good deed pardon me?

LADY.

    And quit all former injury.

SICOPHANT.

    But let me tell your highness, by the way,   1745

    The queen is not so hasty of your death.

LADY.

    No, for she had rather have my life prolonged.

*1741. care] card Q1; Gibbs in Simpson suggests cared. 1744. quit] quite Q1.

    1736. avouch] acknowledge, take the responsibility for.

SICOPHANT.

    I do assure your highness on mine honor,

    When I did say she sent me to destroy you,

    I slandered her great mercy towards you,   1750

    For she had given me order to release you.

LADY.

    Oh monstrous lie!

SICOPHANT.

                Believe it, for 'tis true.

    And this, moreover; she so much repents

    Her former pride and hardness towards you,

    That she could wish it never had been done.   1755

LADY.

    Then I repent me of my wrongs towards her,

    And in the stead of a reward proposed

    To him that should destroy her, I do wish

    Death be his death, that undertakes the deed.

SICOPHANT.

    But will you not forget these princely words   1760

    If alteration should ensue?

LADY.

    Not I, I in my oaths am true.

SICOPHANT.

    Except once more the lords crown Elidure.

[_Moves toward_ Queen _with_ Lady Elidure.]

LADY.

    Though that should chance, I'll hold my promise sure.

SICOPHANT [_aside to_ Queen].

    And you too, madam?

QUEEN [_aside to_ Sicophant].

                   So thou murder'st her.   1765

SICOPHANT [_aside to_ Queen].

    Know that Lord Peridurus and his brother

    Are in the battle slain, and by the nobles

    Her husband Elidure raised to the state.

    Setting aside all jesting, queen, believe it,

    And truce with her, lest she triumph again.   1770

QUEEN [_coming forward_].

    For God's sake make us friends.

SICOPHANT.

    Good Lord, how strange these reconciled foes

    Behold each other!

LADY.

                 Sister.

QUEEN.

                 Kind sister.

SICOPHANT.

    Then make me your brother. Say, are you friends?

1766-67. his brother/Are] his/brother are Q1. 1772-73. foes/Behold] foes be-/hold Q1.

BOTH.

    We are.

SICOPHANT.

          Then chance what can,   1775

    In this I have proved myself an honest man.

                Enter Malgo.

MALGO.

    The king, your husband, madam, new released,

    Desires your presence at his coronation.

LADY.

    My Elidure a third time to be crowned!

MALGO.

    True, madam, and expects your company.   1780

LADY.

    And you knew this before?

SICOPHANT.

                 No, on mine honor.

LADY.

    Neither you, sister?

QUEEN.

                 Neither.

LADY.

                        If you did,

    My oath is past, and what I have lately sworn

    1782. <u>If you did</u>] Even if you did.

I'll hold inviolate. Here all strife ends,
Thy wit has made two proud shrews perfect friends.   1785

Exeunt [omnes].

[xiv]   *Enter in state*, Elidure, Cornwell,
Martianus, Morgan, and all the lords.

CORNWELL.
A third time live our gracious sovereign,
Monarch of England, crowned by these hands.

ELIDURE.
A third time, lords, I do return your love,
And wish it with my soul, so heaven were pleased,
My ambitious brothers had not died for this.   1790
But we have given them honorable graves,

Enter Queen and Lady [Elidure, Malgo,
and Sicophant].

And mourned their most untimely funeral.
My loved queen! Come, seat thee by my side,
Partner in all my sorrows and my joys;
And you, her reconciled sister, sit
By her in second place of majesty.
It joys me that you have outworn your pride.

1784. inviolate] unbroken, intact.
1792. untimely] premature, ill-timed.

LADY.

    Methinks, my gracious husband and my king,

    I never took more pleasure in my glass

    Than I receive in her society.   1800

QUEEN.

    Nor I in all my state as in her love.

                 [Enter messenger.]

ELIDURE.

    My Lord of Cornwell, who's that whispers to you?

    Or what's the news?

CORNWELL.

    My liege, he tells me here's a great contention

    Betwixt two noted persons of the land   1805

    Much spoke of by all states. One Somebody

    Hath brought before your highness and this presence

    An infamous and strange-opinioned fellow

    Called Nobody. They would entreat your highness

    To hear their matters scanned.   1810

ELIDURE.

    We'll sit in person on their controversies.

    Admit them, Cornwell.

    1803. Or] now.
    1806. states] estates.
    1807. presence] an assembly, a company.

LADY.

    Is that strange monster took, so much renowned

    In city, court, and country for lewd pranks?

    'Tis well, we'll hear how he can purge himself.   1815

        Enter Somebody, *bringing in* Nobody *and*

          his man, with bills and staves.

SOMEBODY.

    Now, sirrah, we have brought you before the king,

    Where's your heart now?

NOBODY.

    My heart's in my hose, but my face was never

    ashamed to show itself yet, before king or kaiser.

SOMEBODY.

    And where's your heart, sirrah?   1820

CLOWN.

    My heart's lower than my hose, for mine is at

*1821. is it Q1.

    1814. *lewd pranks*] foolish, ill-mannered tricks of a malicious or mischievous nature.
    1815.2. *staves*] sticks, poles, or clubs used as weapons.
    1817. *heart*] courage.
    1818. *heart's . . . hose*] ludicrous intensification of "the heart sinks," connoting extreme fear; also, because of Nobody's shape (no body), his heart is literally in his hose.
    1819. *kaiser*] an emperor, as a ruler superior to kings.
    1821-22. *at my heel*] he is thus more dejected than Nobody.

my heel. But wheresoever it is, it is a true heart,

and so is not Somebody.

SOMEBODY.

Health to your majesty, and to the queen,

With a heart lower than this humble earth   1825

Whereon I kneel. I beg against this fellow,

Justice, my liege.

ELIDURE.

    Against whom?

SOMEBODY.

      Against Nobody.

NOBODY.

My liege, his words well suit unto his thoughts;

He wishes no man justice, being composed

Of all deceit, of subtlety and slight.   1830

For mine own part, if in this royal presence,

And before all these true judicial lords,

I cannot with sincereness clear myself

Of all suggestions falsely coined against me,

Let me be hanged up sunning in the air,   1835

And made a scarecrow.

MARTIANUS.

Let's hear his accusations,

And then how well thou canst acquit thyself.

SOMEBODY.

    First, when this monster made his residence
    Within the country, and dispersed his shape   1840
    Through every shire and county of the land,
    Where plenty had before a quiet seat,
    And the poor commons of the land were full
    With rich abundance and satiety,
    At his arrive, great dearths and scarcity   1845
    By engrossing corn and racking poor men's rents.
    This makes so many poor and honest farmers
    To sell their leases and to beg their bread;
    This makes so many beggars in the land.

CORNWELL.

    Ay, but what proof or lawful evidence   1850
    Can you bring forth that this was done by him?

SOMEBODY.

    My lord, I traced him, and so found him out.
    But should your lordship not believe my proof,
    Examine all the rich and wealthy chuffs,

*1841. county] country Q1.

    1844. satiety] full satisfaction.
    1846. engrossing] buying up as much of a commodity as possible for the purpose of retailing it at a monopoly price.
    1852. traced] investigated, followed.
    1854. chuffs] misers; rude, coarse fellows.

Whose full-crammed garners to the roofs are filled, 1855
In every dearth who makes this scarcity,
And every man will clearly quit himself.
Then consequently, it must be Nobody.
Base copper money is stamped, the mint disgraced;
Make search who doth this, every man clears one, 1860
So consequently, it must be Nobody.
Besides, whereas the nobles of the land
And gentlemen built goodly manor houses
Fit to receive a king and all his train,
And there kept royal hospitality, 1865
Since this intestine monster Nobody
Dwells in these goodly houses, keeps no train;
A hundred chimneys, and not one cast smoke;
And now the cause of these mock-beggar Halls
Is this: they are dwelt in by Nobody. 1870
For this out of the country he was chased.

*1869. Halls] Hal Q1.

    1859. base] alloyed with less valuable metal; counterfeit.
    1860. every . . . one] each man acquits himself.
    1866. intestine] internal with regard to a country or people.
    1867. keeps no train] he keeps no train.
    1869. mock-beggar Halls] mansions fine without but neglected within, where no hospitality is practiced.

NOBODY.

    My royal liege, why am I thus disgraced?

    I'll prove that sland'rous wretch hath this all done.

ELIDURE.

    'Tis good you can acquit you. Such abuses

    Grow in the country, and unknown to us!   1875

    Nay then, no marvel that so many poor

    Starve in the streets and beg from door to door.

    Then, sirrah, purge you from this country blame,

    Or we will make thee the world's public shame.

CORNWELL.

    Now, Nobody, what can you say to this?   1880

CLOWN [aside].

    My master hath good cards on his side, I'll warrant him.

NOBODY.

    My lord, you know that slanders are no proofs,

    Nor words without their present evidence.

    If things were done, they must be done by Somebody,

    Else could they have no being. Is corn hoarded?   1885

    Somebody hoards it, else it would be dealt

    In mutual plenty throughout all the land.

    Are there rents raised? If Nobody should do it,

    Then should it be undone. Is

*1888. there] their Q1.

    Base money stamped and the king's letters forged?   1890
    Somebody needs must do it, therefore not I.
    And where he says great houses long since built
    Lie destitute, and waste, because inhabited
    By Nobody, my liege, I answer thus:
    If Somebody dwelt therein I would give place.   1895
    Or would he but allow those chimneys fire,
    They would cast clouds to heaven; the kitchen food,
    It would relieve the poor; the cellars beer,
    It would make strangers drink. But he commits
    These outrages, then lays the blame on me,   1900
    And for my good deeds I am made a scorn.
    I only give the tired a refuge seat,
    The unclothed garments, and the starved meat.
CLOWN.
    How say you by this, Master Somebody? I believe
    you will be found out by and by.   1905
CORNWELL.
    If this be true, my liege, as true it is,
    Somebody will be found an arrant cheater,
    Unless he better can acquit himself.
SICOPHANT [<u>aside to</u> Somebody].
    Touch him with the city, since you have taken

    1902. <u>refuge seat</u>] a place to rest.

the foil in the country. 1910
MARTIANUS.
   Sirrah, what can you say to this?
SOMEBODY.
   What should I say, my lord? See here complaints
   Made in the city against Nobody,
   As well as in the country. See their bills;
   Here's one complains his wife hath been abroad, 1915
   And asking where she revels night by night,
   She answers she hath been with Nobody.
   Here's queans maintained in every suburb street;
   Ask who maintains them, and 'tis Nobody.
   Watches are beaten and constables are scoffed 1920
   In dead of night; men are made drunk in taverns;
   Girls lose their maidenheads at thirteen years;
   Pockets picked and purses cut in throngs--
QUEEN.
   Enough, enough! Doth Nobody all this?
   Though he hath cleared himself from country crimes, 1925
   He cannot scape the city.
NOBODY.
               Yes, dread queen,
   I must confess these things are daily done,
   For which I here accuse this Somebody,

1909-10. taken the foil] been repulsed or checked.
1918. queans] strumpets, harlots.

That everywhere with slanders dogs my steps,
And cunningly assumes my borrowed shape. 1930
Women lie out; if they be took and found
With Somebody, then Nobody goes clear,
Else the blame's mine. He doth these faults unknown,
Then slanders my chaste innocence for proof.
Somebody doth maintain a common strumpet 1935
I'th' Garden alleys, and undid himself.
Somebody swaggered with the watch last night,
Was carried to the Counter. Somebody
Once picked a pocket in this playhouse yard,
Was hoisted on the stage and shamed about it. 1940

CLOWN.

Ha ha, hath my master met with you?

NOBODY.

Alas, my liege, your honest Nobody
Builds churches in these days, and hospitals,
Relieves the several prisons in the city,
Redeems the needy debtor from the hole, 1945
And when this Somebody brings infant children

1938-39. Counter. Somebody/Once] counter./somebody once Q1.

1931. lie out] sleep outside their own houses.
1936. I'th'] in the.
1936. Garden alleys] the alleys of Covent Garden, an area notorious as a place of strumpets and stews.
1945. hole] a dungeon; the name of one of the worst apartments in the Counter prison in Wood Street, London.

And leaves them in the night at strangers' doors,
Nobody fathers them, provides them nurses.
What should I say? Your highness' love I crave,
That am all just.
CORNWELL.
                    Then Somebody's a knave. 1950
SICOPHANT [aside to Somebody].
If neither city nor country will prevail,
to him with the court, Master Somebody,
and there you will match him.
SOMEBODY.
Then touching his abuses in the court--
CORNWELL.
Ay, marry, Nobody, what say you to this? 1955
See, here are dangerous libels 'gainst the state,
And no name to them, therefore Nobody's.
MARTIANUS.
Besides, strange rumors and false buzzing tales
Of mutinous leesings raised by Nobody.
MALGO.
False dice and cheating brought even to the
                            presence, 1960
And who dares be so impudently knavish,
Unless some fellow of your name and garb?

1953. match] prove a match for.
1958. buzzing] whispered, muttered.
1959. leesings] losses, destructions.

MORGAN.

> Cards of advantage, with such cheating tricks,
> Brought even amongst the noblest of the land,
> And when these cozening shifts are once discovered,   1965
> There is no cheater found, save Nobody.

SOMEBODY.

> How canst thou answer these?

NOBODY.

> Even as the rest.
> Are libels cast? If Nobody did make them,
> And Nobody's name to them, they are no libels,
> For he that sets his name to any slander,   1970
> Makes it by that no libel. This approves
> He forged those slanderous writs to scandal me.
> And for false cards and dice, let my great slops
> And his big-bellied doublet both be searched,
> And see which harbors most hypocrisy.   1975

QUEEN.

> Let them both be searched.

SICOPHANT.

> I'll take my leave of the presence.

1971. approves] <u>Gibbs in Simpson suggests proves.</u>

   1973. <u>slops</u>] wide baggy breeches or hose.

CLOWN.

    Nay, Master Sicophant, we'll have the inside of
your pockets translated too; we'll see what
stuffing they have; I'll take a little pains   1980
with you.

ELIDURE.

    What have you there in Nobody's pockets?

CORNWELL.

    Here are, my liege, bonds forfeit by poor men,
Which he released out of the usurers hands
And canceled. Leases likewise forfeited,   1985
By him repurchased. These petitions
Of many poor men to prefer their suits
Unto your highness.

ELIDURE.

                    Thou art just, we know;
All great men's pockets should be lined so.

QUEEN.

    What bombast bears his gorge?   1990

MARTIANUS.

    False cards, false dice;
The king's hand counterfeit;

1991. Simpson assigns to Mor.

    1979. translated] turned inside out.
    1990. bombast] padding, stuffing.
    1990. gorge] here used to mean large stomach.

>   Bonds put in suit to gain the forfeitures;
>
>   Forged deeds to cheat men of their ancient land,
>
>   And thousand such like trash. 1995

CLOWN.

>   Nay, look you here; here's one that for his bones
>
>   is prettily stuffed. Here's fulhams and gourds; here's
>
>   tall men and low men; here trey-deuce-ace,
>
>   passage comes apace.

SOMEBODY.

>   Mercy, great king!

SICOPHANT.

>   Mercy, my sovereign! 2000

CORNWELL.

>   My liege, you cannot be too severe in punishing
>
>   Those monstrous crimes, the only stain and blemish
>
>   To the weal public.

*2001. be too] to be Q1.

    1996. bones] dice.
    1997. gourds] a kind of false dice.
    1998. tall men and low men] dice so loaded as to turn up high or low numbers only respectively.
    1998-99. trey-deuce-ace . . . apace] a difficult passage. The proverbial phrase "ere you can say trey-ace" means quickly. Also a trey-ace is a throw that turns up trey with one die and ace with the other; hence trey-deuce-ace may be a throw of three dice, or here a reference to three dice loaded to turn up in this sequence. A passage can be a fight or verbal altercation, and the clown may be referring to this as a result of using crooked dice.
    2003. weal public] the general interest or good of the public.

ELIDURE.
>   Villains, hear your doom:
  Thou that hast been the oppression of the poor,
  Shalt be more poor than penury itself;   2005
  All that thou hast is forfeit to the law;
  For thy extortion I will have thee branded
  Upon the forehead with the letter F;
  For cheating, whipped; for forging, lose thine ears;
  Last, for abasing of thy sovereign's coin   2010
  And trait'rous impress of our kingly seal,
  Suffer the death of traitors. Bear him hence.

SOMEBODY.
  Since I must needs be martyred, grant me this:
  That Nobody may whip, or torture me,
  Or hang me for a traitor.

MORGAN.
>   Away with him.   2015

SOMEBODY.
  Or if needs I must die a traitor's death,
  That Nobody may see me when I die.

MALGO.
  Hence with the traitor.   [Exit Somebody, guarded.]

2008. _F_] meaning felon.
2013. martyred] tormented, mutilated.

CLOWN.

    I know by your complexion you were ripe for the

    hangman, but now to this lean gentleman.   2020

LADY.

    Let me doom him: smooth spaniel, soothing groom,

    Slick oily knave, egregious parasite,

    Thou turning vane and changing weathercock,

    My sentence is thou shalt be naked stripped,

    And by the city beadles soundly whipped.   2025

CLOWN.

    I'll make bold to see th'execution.

NOBODY.

    Well hath the king decreed. Now, by your

    highness' patience, let Nobody borrow a word or

    two of everybody.

The Epilogue.

Here if you wonder why the king, Elidurus, bestows   2030

nothing on me for all my good services in his

land--if the multitude should say he hath

    2019-20. complexion . . . hangman] a personal appearance that suggests a tendency toward crime and therefore a justification for hanging. cf. Shakespeare, Measure for Measure, IV.ii.34-5.
    2021. soothing] flattering.
    2026. make bold] venture, presume so far as.

preferred Nobody, Somebody or other would say it
were not well done, for in doing good to Nobody
he should but get himself an ill name. Therefore 2035
I will leave my suit to him, and turn to you.
Kind gentlemen, if anybody here dislike Nobody, then
I hope Everybody have pleased you, for being
offended with Nobody, nor anybody can find
himself aggrieved. Gentlemen, they have a cold 2040
suit that have Nobody to speak in their cause,
and therefore blame us not to fear. Yet our
comfort is this: if Nobody have offended, you
cannot blame Nobody for it, or rather we will
find Somebody hereafter shall make good the 2045
fault Nobody hath done; and so I crave the
general grace of everybody.

ELIDURE.

Now forward, lords, long may our glories stand,
Three sundry times crowned king of this fair land.

Exeunt.

FINIS.

2039. nor] Q1; *Simpson suggests* not.

2142. *blame . . . fear*] the meaning is unclear; perhaps do not impute our actions to fear.

Appendix

28. wit's] both <u>wit's</u> and <u>wits</u> are possible. If <u>wits</u> is accepted, "are" is understood in the phrase <u>your wits green</u>, and Cornwell is talking to both brothers. <u>Wit's</u> however is directed only to Vigenius, and given Vigenius' address in line 27, it is more likely that Cornwell is speaking to Vigenius rather than to both.

220. Cornwell's] because of the reference to Devonshire in the same line, Cornwall seems intended, and I have modernized the spelling on this basis.

302. masques] the quarto spelling <u>masks</u> is a possible reading in this context, but <u>masks</u> is also a variant spelling of <u>masques</u>. I choose the form <u>masques</u> because it is parallel to the other terms in the line, while <u>masks</u> is not.

419. a bout] I have found no use of the word <u>about</u> in a similar context. To <u>dare about</u> with someone seems a possible reading, but there is no evidence that the phrase was ever used. Hence the simplest and most likely explanation for the term here is that the compositor read the two words <u>a</u> and <u>bout</u> as one in the copy text. Cf. similar misreadings in lines 883 and 1998.

560. a midst] the spelling <u>amidsts</u> has no recognized meaning. The <u>s</u> was printed by some unexplained accident.

658. body] the playwright is almost certainly referring to the fable of the belly and the rebellious body parts (cf. <u>Coriolanus</u>, I.i.99-167). However it is unlikely that the compositor would have misread <u>body</u> for <u>belly</u>, or that body was accidentally printed for <u>belly</u>. In spite of the fact that neither word fits the image well, the probable conclusion is that the playwright intended the reading <u>body</u>, and that he had simply not remembered the fable accurately.

714. revert] the <u>r</u> was probably dropped accidentally in composition, as <u>revet</u> has no recognized meaning. Simpson's choice fits the passage and stresses the changing positions of the two women throughout the play.

716. Dejected] the quarto reading is clearly in error, and Simpson's suggestion is probable, given the fact that in printing the character i also stood for j, and Sicophant's later use of this term in a similar context (l. 1035).

883. with all] as in line 419, the compositor apparently read with all as one word in his copy text. Withall makes little sense here, and the hyperbole of with all the world fits in the context and tone of this scene.

891. And have more] this is the only major press variant in the quarto copies collated. The sense of the passage suggests that have should be retained. In addition, even though the meter is quite irregular throughout the play, the closing couplet of a speech is generally regular, and here the retention of have produces that regularity.

903. am a slave] I accept Simpson's reading on the basis of sense, the balance it creates in the line, and meter.

1029. This line is in keeping with the constant shifting of positions of the two women throughout the play, but here Lady Elidure is up and the Queen is undergoing the pains. Hence the line should be assigned to the Queen, and was probably misaligned by the compositor.

1052. Oh] I have been unable to discover the meaning of the caret over the o in the quarto, but I note it because it does not seem to be a stray mark or an accident.

1149. heavy] Simpson's suggestion seems accurate. No meaning of heaven seems appropriate here, and the compositor probably set heaven due to an eye skip from line 1146.

1361. lanes] no meaning of lands fits the passage, and lanes is probable, given the other direct objects of the sentence. The error might have come about because of an eye skip from line 1355, but that is a bit unlikely. The compositor probably confused the character e with d, an easy orthographic mistake.

1368. The Queen and Lady Elidure are clearly matched combatants throughout the play. Peridure is concerned with being king, while the Queen is concerned with dominating Lady Elidure. Hence it is much more in character for the Queen to speak this line than for Peridure to do so. In addition, the balanced, one line structure that characterizes the speeches of Vigenius and Peridure in similar situations in the play (ll. 265-67, 1669-70) is here preserved by assigning this line to the Queen.

1627. catch] I have been unable to find evidence of a construction of a future and past tense that would allow catcht, and catch seems to be the least complicated and most logical alternative.

1634. thy] the contention here is over which claim to the throne shall stand; hence for emphasis Peridure is saying my claim shall endure, and thy claim shall not. Thy also parallels the use of thy in line 1635, and the error is most readily explained by foul case.

1670. PERIDURE] Elidure is not in the scene, and the speech clearly belongs to Peridure, as he and Vigenius are exchanging challenges. The quarto reading Elid. is an unexplained accident.

1688. changes] charges is a possible reading, but no meaning of the word makes particularly good sense in this line. I therefore incline to Gibbs' reading, as changes does fit the general theme of the play and of the couplet, and can be readily explained by foul case, or perhaps even a misreading of r for n in the copy text.

1741. care] Gibb's suggestion is possible, but creates an unusual form of the verb not found anywhere else in the play. A misreading of d for e is equally possible, and is strengthened by a similar misreading in line 1361.

1821. is] there is no reason to retain the quarto reading it, as the word makes little sense in this position. It was probably set here due to foul case, as it seems unlikely that the compositor would have confused the two characters.

1841. county] since the sense here demands that the term used be parallel to shire and of a smaller size than land, county seems intended, with country having been set by mistake because of an eye skip from line 1840.

1869. Halls] throughout the passage concerning the manor houses Somebody is speaking in the plural, and even though Elizabethan practice did not always require consistent agreement, the plural is intended here as shown by the adjective these and the pronoun they. The compositor may have misread his copy text, or the s may have been accidentally dropped during printing.

1888. there] the quarto reading their is a possible reading, but because all other subjects in the passage are general in nature, I choose the alternate spelling there for this text, since it maintains this general concern, as opposed to their which is specific.

2001. be too] the quarto reading makes little sense, and the compositor has simply inverted the word order.